For Dave
Physics is so
(don't understand
But Thanks !
Martin

Poems for the Young at Heart

Also by Martin Stannard:

Baffled in Nacton (Greylag Press) 1983
The Flat of the Land (Wide Skirt Press) 1987
Something Cold and White (Bad Seed Press) 1987
The Gracing of Days: New & Selected Poems (Slow Dancer) 1989
Denying England (Wide Skirt Press) 1989
From A Recluse To A Roving I Will Go (The Shed) 1993. Full colour artist's book, in large
   format, produced in collaboration with printmaker Dale Devereux Barker
Easter (Waldean Press) 1994
A Hundred Of Happiness and Other Poems (Smith/Doorstop) 1995
Two Sides of a One-Sided Conversation (Dog) 1996
Conversations with Myself : Selected Reviews and Notes 1984-1998 (Stride) 1999
Difficulties and Exultations (Smith/Doorstop) 2001
Writing Down the Days: New & Selected Poems (Stride) 2001
Poems on Various Subjects (Shoestring Press) 2001
How To Live A Life (The Shed) 2002. Limited edition art book in collaboration with Dale
Devereux Barker
Coral (Leafe Press) 2004
Faith (Shadowtrain Books) 2010
How To Live A Life: Selected Uncollected Poems 2002-2009 (Argotist eBooks) 2010
Respondings: Selected Reviews & Notes 2004-2007 (Argotist eBooks) 2011

Poems for the Young at Heart

Martin Stannard

Acknowledgements:

Some of these poems, or slightly different versions of them, first appeared in the following publications either in print or online (or both): Litter, Shadowtrain, Stride, The Echo Room, The North; and/or on the blog of Rupert Mallin (http://mallin.blogspot.ca/) and at August 1, 2013 (http://augustone2013.blogspot.co.uk/)

Bits of them may also have first appeared in some shape or form as "Notations" at One Million Elephants Couldn't Begin To Understand (http://martinstannard.com/elephants/), which continues to be updated daily.

Author's website: http://martinstannard.com/

Published by Leafe Press
Nottingham, England

www.leafepress.com

ISBN 978-0-9574048-4-7

CONTENTS

(PROLOGUE)

ONE WEEK IN THE LIFE

OCCASIONAL POEMS

(PROLOGUE)

When you were born I was not.
When I was born you were already old.
My love, I regret being born so late
and your being born so early.

When you were born I was not.
When I was born you were already old.
My love, I hate not being born the same time
as you, unable to enjoy the sharing of days.

When I was born you, my love, were not.
When you were born I was already old.
I was far from you, on the other side of the world,
separated by land and sea.

When I was born you, my love, were not.
When you were born I was already old.
I long to be a butterfly, seeking out flowers
and resting every night upon fragrant grasses.

Tongguanyao (Tonguan kiln) "porcelain poem"
inscribed on porcelain pot, Tang Dynasty (618–907)
discovered in Changsha, Hunan, China
author unknown

trans. MS, July 2012

One Week In The Life

1. PANDORA

Friday. Tomorrow the mail wagon arrives from town.
I'm expecting a letter from Pandora.
I hope she has managed to seal that hog deal we spoke of.

> The fields are filled
> with young winter wheat.
> Johnson is spraying herbicide
> to control weeds.
> Why are you even asking?

But the windmill has blown away and taken the miller
with it. He will not be missed: we have not eaten local bread
since before the third of the five great corporate bodies
landed on us and painted all the cottages beige.

I can picture our local poet standing in Old Meadow
thinking about his rusty bicycle with tears in his eyes
before he plods his weary way homeward to his cat and fireside
and an evening writing about when his bicycle was a horse.

> We're nearing the end
> of one year and the beginning
> of another; we shall have to
> wait and see if there is
> any improvement.

Some of us are watching the skies.
Pandora if she were here would say to abandon superstition
and to grab our pencils and get up a petition.

2. EVENTIDE

Saturday eventide. The mail wagon came from town today
but brought only bills and something to burn from the bank.
There is no word from Pandora; I think I am getting a bit of a cold.

> I had planned to clean
> out the gutters before
> the bad weather sets in.

Instead I went to see Grandmother Simms
for one of her herbal remedies. We all swear by them:
recovery and pleasant dream-filled sleep in an old wine bottle.
I came away with a tea of elderflower and peppermint
and a bag of leaves: thyme and rosemary.

> From my window at twilight
> I saw a long-legged white bird
> perched on the gatepost.

I have no idea what it was. Pandora would have taken down
the *Popular Ornithology* and searched until she found it.
But she is not here. She is in town thinking about being here.

3. CHURCH

Sunday. I should be in church but increasingly
church-going seems to be little more than a futile gesture
and with the weather turning colder and damper I am going
to sit and watch the trees standing barely, barely able to stand.

>   One place to be in the world
>   is the fireside with its flames and its heat
>   and all it reminds us of.

They say that in town on Sundays people hold festivals
and entertainments we do not have words fit to describe;
some even say how drunkenness and lechery are encouraged
by the government so people forget how unhappy they are.

>   The world is full of words
>   some of which can be believed and some
>   which can barely be credited.

Pandora will be in her lodgings and thinking about
being here. If sounds of drunkenness and lechery reach her ears
she will stop them with the waxen ear plugs
I made for her and continue to read from my letters.

4. CARRIER DOVE

Monday. A carrier dove has bought a note from Pandora
to say she is lonely in town among its indifferent people.

> Her loneliness
> translates into a sadness
> we share.

Here there is a constant drizzle, even the fish
are lethargic and morose. In the byre
the cattle low their indifference to all things.

I went for a long walk today across the fields to see
if I could reach the horizon. The attempt has been made
many times but has always ended in failure.

> Today was no
> exception as the horizon
> kept its distance.

I intend sending a message back to Pandora by return dove
but it's perched on a rafter and refuses to come down.

5. SUFFOCATION AND RESCUE

Tuesday. I was kept awake most of the night by high winds
rattling the door chains and window frames forcing complaints
from the livestock. It will be no surprise to find trees down.

In brief intervals of sleep my dreams were of suffocation
and rescue. As is the way of dreams they were inexplicable
insofar as they could be remembered at all.

> There is no connection
> between what I suppress
> and what I express.
>
> They are saying in the village
> I spend too much time
> alone for my own good.

I inspected the orchard and found little wind damage beyond
leaf fall and one snapped bough off the plum tree. But
the glasshouse has lost its glass; it's nowhere to be found.

The same gale that blows around my head disturbs also
the hair of Pandora in the town. Brick walls and glass towers
do not divide us. Rather we are held together by their shadows.

6. WIND REPLACED BY RAIN

Wednesday. Wind replaced by rain. The geese sheltered under the trees
in the lane. The High Street was awash. Outside Wedlock's the Butcher
there was a canoe lashed to the roof-rack of a mud-spattered Volvo estate.

My Wellington boots have seen a good deal of wear and tear but
they have some years left in them yet. Those extra pounds splashed
out for the Superior Countryman™ have long since proved their worth.

> The farmers say
> money is useful
> if you want to buy a cow
>
> but if you don't want
> to buy a cow
> it will only attract robbers
>
> (A hat! You cannot live here without a good hat.)
>
> so its best to spend it on
> something. A new smock
> may look good
>
> but you will be unfulfilled.
> Some of them go to dives
> in town to be fulfilled.

On the hat-rack in the hall Pandora's Panama hangs awaiting her
homecoming head. In a storm sometimes a hat can be a liability; we have
all seen the fat farmer chasing his fedora futilely across a fallow field.

> The weather vane on the church steeple is motionless but dripping.
> Gravestones glisten wetly as I weave my witless way between them
> on my short-cut home with a carrier bag of what might be road-kill.

7. WATCHING CATTLE

I like to watch cattle. The beauty of cows. Steam
rising from their flanks in the autumn sunshine.
The winter feed is in the sheds. It's Thursday and

     Pandora is returned.

The landscape is constantly changing. Shops close down.
We drive the cart to the hypermarket on the edge of town.
Days are so short at this time of year we are starved of light.

     Pandora is not staying.

My afternoon boots bring home half the muddy fields
from their trudge. Such heavy feet I have. Downhill is uphill.
Tools rust from disuse. Sometimes it is hard to leave the house.

     Pandora is returned
     but she is not staying.

     I am frozen.
     I am prescient.

Tonight the Johnson's barn will burn to the ground.
It will be blamed on one of the gangs from town.
There is something wrong with me. There is evil. It exists.

Occasional Poems

3 OPENINGS

1.

The tall man opened the door and

2.

The tall handsome man opened his eyes and

3.

The tall handsome but ill-advised man opened the can of worms and

AN ALBATROSS IS PERCHED ON MY SHOULDER

Ever since the Ancient Mariner shot the albatross
I've been sad, but only on days with either an A or an
      M in them.
There do not seem to have been many happy dAys since 1798.
Also of late I've been suffering from what I hear is "auditory fatigue"
which loosely translated means I so am fed up listening to
      anything,
but primarily to people talking, and primarily people talking too
too loud. Oh sea! Your incessant song is,
or would be if you were in earshot, the only sound tolerable these days,
for you know everything about how my heart beats
whenever the future I consider. But hush!

Censorship (which I totally deplore, by the way) will not let me tell
      you
who am I, but nothing else about me is secret. My book an open heart,
my heart an open sore, and an open sore is not very nice
because it attracts the worst kind of plague and
pestilence. This reminds me of London, 1665,
and I remember I was looking forward to the 1790s and the arrival of
      Romanticism
 and one day I was in harbour awaiting a vessel
(a ship upon which to sail into oblivion's sunset) and a chap asked
because I had an albatross perched on my shoulder "Why?"
and I gave him the only reply possible:
an albatross is perched on my shoulder because he likes it.

A HAPPY AND PROSPEROUS LIFE

You asked me if I was happy
but instead of answering your question
I spent the next I don't know how long
analyzing it and your blonde hair
turned to a wispy silver-grey and the day
turned into one long period of thought
like when you suggested we could either
turn into stone and wait to be gazed upon
by people with nothing better to do
or take to the air like the Wright Brothers
who in 1903 took to the air in the manner
of men doing something altogether new
and I considered the choices for
I don't know how long until the birds
hiding in the trees shed their feathers
and fell to the ground stunned
to find themselves imagined doing
anything as bizarre as falling to anything.

It was the afternoon of the next day
and on receipt of my letter ("It is with regret
I must inform you that I can no longer.....")
you uttered the words "I am crushed" and
I too was crushed and smashed and splattered
against the walls of my private space
its stars scattered like tiny jewels hurled
against the wall of a boudoir in a novel
by Constance Small queen of timeless romance
as if to prove it's ridiculous to be sentimental
when everyone you love is on a train away
never to come back in a month of Sundays.

I didn't want to move house: house was
firmly rooted in the past and the past is
as valuable as the future might turn out to be
if ever it arrives and more room is always
only a bigger vacancy in which to prove oneself
unfit for purpose here comes a simile which
is like being the law of gravity crashing to earth
and the collapse of a very small civilization
nobody knew was there until someone

stumbled upon what had been left behind:
a load of unread books some unfinished poems
and what appeared to be an ancient manuscript
setting out a schedule to ensure a happy
and prosperous life. Yes, I said
a schedule to ensure a happy and prosperous life.

BLESSED

Jesus, I've shifted so many units recently
blessèd I am become. Take my picture before
I explode all over myself. I'm going to go
up a mountain with my team-mates. I don't
want to go but if I don't I'll be down here and
they'll be up there and it's a gap I can't afford.
Sometimes *this life pisses me off* so much:
it's the opposite of what I want, of who I am.

I hate serious. Please cosmetic me up until
divine sleepiness engulfs me. I have assumed
a certain shape but I don't know if I'll ever be
happy with it. *I'm drinking too much wine*
and I just fell off my chair but it's not a high one.

Shallow are the waters in which I'll drown,
and if anyone cares good luck to them. My lips
are blue because I like them that way but
if you try to paint me I'll set the dogs on you.
I have two dogs. One of them wants to eat
the other, but it's against all the rules.

Jesus, I've fallen foul of all my best intentions
but *I'm too drunk to think* of the consequences
and the boulders are tumbling down the mountain
taking my team-mates with them. *I care* but I
don't care. Sometimes I think I should care more
but sometimes this life pisses me off so much
caring seems inappropriate. I'm going to go
and have my nails done, and feel briefly blessed.

CARRIE DAINFORTH

Sometimes I sleep.

Last night I dreamed of Carrie Dainforth
and the creation of castles
but see what falls by the wayside
when the day arrives with its darkness.

And I don't know what's worse:
how she refuses to go away
or how she refuses to come to life.

DESIGN FLAW

The doctor says my back ache (DESIGN FLAW) is a sign of tension
and worry but common sense says it's a sign of a bad back. I suggest
a public enquiry: that should get to the bottom of things. Sun

beating down on my feathers is overpowering (DESIGN FLAW) – one wishes
that wings would allow one to fly, and not prove to be such a burden.
How come the sky, for all its airy allure, is so far away? If one could choose

a state in which to survive would it be filled with such storm and stress?
And should one begin a sentence with a word forbidden by grammarians
and pedants (DESIGN FLAW)? God knows. I'm stretched stretched out on

my massage girl's thing upon which her clients stretch out and I can
feel the tension ebbing away and increasing all at the same time,
which is called a paradox, and sometimes a "DESIGN FLAW", my mind being

floored (DESIGN FLAWED) as when a boxer (the pugilist, not the dog) hits
the deck (not a deck as upon a ship, one means the canvas, not the canvas
upon which an artist paints, one means the floor of the ring, not

the ring one places upon the finger of one's betrothed (DESIGN FLAW),
but the ring within which the pugilists pugil) (where was I? Oh yes…)
my mind being floored – an occurrence so common one is tempted

to suggest there's a design flaw somewhere in there: one wishes wings
would open the door to flight, and not prove so burdensome, bringing
one down so often to the level of the ordinary (DESIGN FLAW) mortal.

DOMBEY AND SON

For breakfast the maid brings
the 9th monthly installment of
Dombey and Son and I take it
with a cup of coffee as the China sun
pours itself in through the window
and when I finally disentangle myself
from my nighttime entanglements
and realize swearing about the man
in the next building with the jackhammer
is not going to make him go away
I turn to Otis Redding for soul balm

but there is no soul balm in solitude
and today's plans are in a heap of ruins now
James is gone to Japan which seems
an extravagant way to avoid seeing someone
you could just close your eyes or feign blindness
and Li Min's absence is such emptiness

and so taking a few moments after lunch
to think about where the novel is going
and distracted by the enormous light
pressing through the drapes
(it reminds me of Spain
although I have never been to Spain
where the painter is putting the finishing touches
to a torero putting the finishing touches
to a bull; it is an art and appalling)
it is apparent the novel is entering a new chapter
but I do so dislike contrived metaphors
and I am waiting for Li Min to come home

EPICS OF OPTIMISM

We, the scribblers of hope, burdened by unrelenting sunlight,
have longed to say something you will listen to
and scrawl our words on scraps of paper or type them neatly
so they are readable and easy to understand.

In awe of the soaring spaces of aeroplane heavens
propelled one would think by endless energy and enthusiasm
tuned into a station plausibly wheezy with breathlessness
we are writing our epics addressed to optimism.

Among the pleasures of the road up ahead we expect
the openings of for example marvellous boutiques of shells
and brightly-coloured plastic by glistening celebrities
fervently umbrella'd with luminosity absent any penumbra.

Unencumbered days, we are in constantly silly love
with all our hours enchanted by so many smiling teeth
it's as if all the toothpaste commercials from television
were compressed into one immense and wonderful life.

Our epics of optimism roll along concretely. I am so happy
I don't know what time it is, or phase of the moon, I'm even
over the moon to find almost fresh lettuce in the refrigerator
and enough water in the tank this evening to fill a bath.

Kitty is fine now, too, all her misplaced baubles having been
located. And finally she has accepted the wonders of science
do not contradict the existence of a deity, as well as the fact that
the bicycle is a natural evolution of the horse into the modern world.

Let me introduce you to the sky and its cotton wool clouds.
Over there is a flotation device wrapped around a salivating child
and there is a gem of geometric precision, a-sparkle at each point,
and there is a swan processing its marvel into the infinite distance.

But what you want to know is does the top of the tree actually
touch the sky, am I right? The answer is what you want it to be
and if your heart is in the right place it will never be the same
twice. By the way, the tree is your friend and so is the sky.

Do not be concerned if there are more answers than questions.
The number of questions is greater than you can imagine
and the methods by which we enjoy them increases as we grow
closer to ourselves and approach the lighter than light.

It is incumbent upon us to contest each negative emotion
but nobody claims this is easy to do although once you understand
the sheer weight of enjoyment to be gained overcoming them
it will be impossible to go back to hiding abed curled up like a baby.

The days when moss grew between our shoulder blades
and bats visited us for darkened conversations at night are over.
We, the scribes of brightness, will write our epics of optimism
in defiance of our true feelings which have always to be concealed.

Majesty must be defiant. Glorious sunrise manufactured by window
salesmen, shovel-loads of glamour, parental advice noted but gleefully
ignored. Yes, we have read the leaflet you gave us and we admire
your ambition but deride its scale, which is nothing like large enough.

Summer is coming, you know, and we are planning to serenade you
with elegant phrases to massage the inside of your mind
because to be comfortable in your skin is angelic, warrior, bejewelled
by baubles, and all white and hot passions pleasurably nurtured.

Always be grateful, by the way, for any gift of music or lyrical grace,
blessings granted by an idea way beyond us. Nothing can take
our beauty and its appurtenances away unless we close our brains.
All we need now is for the choir to wake up to make our joy complete.

We, the scribblers of hope, having longed for so long to say
something you will listen to and understand, scrawl our words
on scraps of paper or type them neatly so they are readable
and we will assemble them later to form our epics of optimism.

FOR MARK HALLIDAY

Mark has asked me to write a poem
that is both comprehensible and moving and
because my middle name is Obliging I am happy
to oblige although the last time I wrote
a comprehensible poem my fan club threatened
to buy a suitcase and fill it full of underwear
and leave me. It took more than an hour
to console her with moves learned from films.

It would be good and surprising to write something
both comprehensible and moving and even rhyming
but I'm not sure it's possible these days to be surprising
or if I'm up to the challenge; anyway, the timing
is all wrong: I just checked the mirror and its going
to be another bad hair day as far as I can see
(which is only into the future and what it's going to be).

For a poem to be both comprehensible and moving
it has to be about something and not merely
a potpourri of words assembled purely for the fun
and pleasantly enjoyable pleasure of it, and that
something has to be of interest to the reader not only
the writer if that is at all possible which it may not
in my case be because I am a selfish kind of poet
and the only enjoyment I really care for is my own.

And anyway what is there but life? and the only life
I know anything about is mine although it's true
I don't find it either comprehensible or moving
merely frustrating and worrying and I cannot imagine
it being of interest to anyone else either living or dead
or (which is more likely) a figment of my imagination.

Once upon a time I wrote a poem someone described
as a futile attempt to explain the unexplainable
but they had misunderstood my intention which was
to write a poem that was a futile attempt to explain
the unexplainable and was in its own wonderful way
a success at the same time as it sang of its own failure,

and this I still find an achievement of which I'm proud.
But it was not moving, and neither is this. Rather
it's a statement of desire and pessimism laced
with a strong dose of defiance. Defiance of what I am
not sure, but without defiance there can be no
hope of fulfilment, and without fulfilment
there is only dismay and a crushing disappointment.

FOUR POEMS

1.

Linger a moment, and let's think about where we are.
And before we linger let's pause a while
to consider how we came to be here.

Some of us took a train, others one day woke up
and discovered somehow their place had been decided for them.
What discoveries they had unwittingly passed by!
You might have been enchanted by back gardens and terraces
and hypnotized by curtainless dens and whores' duvets.

And then some have been dragged here by people who know
what's good for them. One cannot help but admire those who know
what's best and what's right but it never ceases to confound our leaders
how, no matter how many signs they put up, apathy reigns,
and if it's not apathy it's a terribly effective way of doing nothing.

2.

We swim into the study area being transformed into a lagoon
by workmen from the countryside. There is a debate concerning
whether or not electricity is necessary or would it be a luxury
not worth the expense and the complication of forcing it through
eternities of form-filling and bribery and, after all of that, water.

And when the trees topple in a storm an entire army of workers
is flown in to stand them up again. But when an old lady is blown over
everyone stands around discussing the benefits of an early death.

The modernization of our living space continues apace.
It would be pleasant to be able to open the windows but this is only
a theory; there is always the risk of fresh air coming into the room
and sound leaving it, and we prefer to keep our noises to ourselves.

3.

Today (or was it yesterday) there was an organized outing
to the hospital to have our ears put through their paces. I would have
considered going there on horseback, it being more picturesque.
The bus possesses no romance, and it's not even fast.

But horses could not be procured, this being the age of coal.
I told the doctor, I told it, I said the only time my head hurts
is when you poke around inside it with your poking stick.
I'm looking forward to the days when your stick is a thing of the past.

The doctor, it was a woman, this being a time when women can be,
she said how it was only by being done cruel to that a man could
ever hope to start learning what his place in the world was,
and I went home with my ears in a bag and some pills to swallow.

4.

I don't want to bore you but there is institutionalized racism,
sexism and corruption in every corner here. Even when we
eulogize butterflies we are imagining them either pinned to a board
or fluttering their last gasp as we bulldoze their living quarters.
Some people also want to have sex with them, unless they are
white butterflies, which are not exotic enough. I don't know how
things came to this pass: one moment we were outsiders
eyeing the landscape from afar and then before we knew it
we were here, directing daily operations from behind a desk.

It's a hell of a desk, too. A family could live under it, and horses
graze within its shadow. When I lay on it with my head resting on a book
it's as if there is nothing to do in the whole world of life but enjoy
being better than others, and not pitying their pathetic facilities.

GREAT POEM

It has always been one of my ambitions to write a great poem
of the sea. And now as if from out of nowhere appears
a sentence that could be uttered by no-one but a salty sailor:
"Ropes and pulleys are connected to the sea's infrastructure
and gulls and terns perch on the spars of a sailing ship
to watch the unravelling of the disaster that's bound to happen."

Ma's excited by the prospect of a great poem of the sea
but perhaps this will instead become a great poem of the storm.
At this point it's difficult to speak with confidence except to say
typhoons aren't the only upheavals that twist my brain
into a perplexing puzzle the convolutions of which befuddle me.

I am sitting becalmed now, thinking about writing a great poem
either of the sea or of the storm. The haphazardness
of these bouts of genius may signify an unsettled constitution
or the will of a vengeful God. I have no preference either way.

"Ropes and pulleys are connected to the sea's infrastructure
and gulls and terns perch on the spars of a sailing ship
to watch the unravelling of the disaster that's bound to happen"
are pretty okay opening lines and I should be able to find material
to hang on them if I don't think about things too much and
be overwhelmed by my desire to write a great poem of the sea.

(I have decided to stick with the sea because I know little
about it, whereas I am on intimate terms with the storm
and intermittent bouts of over-drinking that prompt
minor cataclysms and summon various horned demons
and, well, I've lost count of the troubles if you want to know.
I think there's nothing interesting left to say about the storm.)

The trouble is control is sometimes lacking.
"A cart loaded with crates of vegetables careers
through the back alleys and swings around corners
so fast the wheels fall off and it smashes into a wall
and we're watching it on our phones in Starbucks"
has just appeared in front of me and it has nothing to do
with the sea or the storm, and I have no desire to write
a great poem about whatever this sentence is about.

I'm going to cross all that out and persevere with my dream
of writing a great poem of the sea. I shall try and avoid
obvious symbolism and other predictable rhetorical moves
and stun readers with unexpected and elegant maritime language
and a 21st century detachment that will move them to tears.
This may seem hugely ambitious, but I refuse to deny myself.

HAMLET

A village without a church of its own
belonging to the parish of another village or town.

1.

My heart is inhabited by some brand of snow fox
but I don't think animals care who they live with
so long as food and drink and absence of cruelty
is the deal. Sunshine seems to be as much like
a fiddler's music as anything else, and when
the owls I bought yesterday afternoon have found
their wings it'll be pretty much business as usual:
entrancing girls will be welcome but won't come.

Fortune, as much a fiend as a vixen, or so I've learned
from my inextensive and inexhaustive researches,
goes round and around in circles or egg-shapes
and everything turns out pear-shaped, which is curiously
interesting, don't you think? The bear just shipped in
from perhaps the Himalayan foothills (I don't know)
is finding his way around:
I wish he wouldn't eat the books;
I wish he wouldn't ravish the slavey;
I wish he wouldn't do anything.

2.

Conflicting accounts of what I just wrote are coming in:
(shall we rest for a while
and listen to a Sting record?
Oh okay, fair enough.)
some people hold that while Ophelia is sprawled bawling
at the bottom of the stairs I'm the psychoanalyst
who doesn't give a damn about how she feels; others
contend that what I saw I only think I saw and what I said
I didn't really mean when I said it. Well, Horatio,
there's a damn sight more to this than meets the eye;
at least, that's what I think I've come to believe.

HOW I WATCH A YEAR GO BY

I would try to spend Summer in my head
then discover I have a head of Winter. I must
have a head of Winter because snow
covers my hair, or my hair is snow, and ice forms
where a smile should be, or people
toboggan down my face and clamber up the back of
my neck in their heavy boots. Birds
who used to nest behind my ears appear
to have abandoned me for sunnier climes. Now

it's time to ditch this laboured metaphor
and embrace simplicity. It's December, or January,
or February – it's so impossible to tell the difference
between one enemy and another, with their lidless eyes
and darkness drugs! It's impossible to do anything
during an Ice Age, although I once wrote a poem
about a hat, or that had a hat in it, a hat for Winter, but
I digress, and already it's windy March, blown in
on the noon tide and a wife's breath with nothing

to commend it but kites and scarves blowing.
This reminds me how once upon a time
a long time ago I was a child, and I flew a kite
and wore a scarf and was blown by the wind into
the path of an oncoming steamroller which, fortunately,
was going very very slowly and I had time not
only to get out of its way but also to read a chapter of
Swallows and Amazons which is not a book
I would like now but I liked then and always
carried around with me in spite of its improbable
weight and Oh suddenly suddenly

suddenly April! here it is with its "the First" and showers
of showerings. I always associate the month of April
with renewal (*Easter*) and renewal with library books
(especially a book of anecdotes, especially one about how
one day a man was getting on a bus and left his left foot
behind on the road; an unexpected uncontrolled dog was

somehow involved and a brouhaha ensued; I mis-
remember the details). May my memory improve! But

it won't, for age encroaches and devours. And here
is May, as it happens, breathing hot and cold but not at
the same time. And all at once I am waking
to phantasmagorias! The wondrous of everything and blissful
excitement of all. Shape alongside a sensation to touch.
Reading and re-building the *Selected Homes of Kate O'Mara*,
prospect of plum in my mouth excellent fruitful times, so much
so incoherence follows. What a time of the year! Summer
must be coming, the flags are fluttering and
I feel almost foreign. For reasons unfathomable

the transition from May to June proves most difficult. They
have different names and weathers but although it's possible
to love both it's impossible to be faithful to either, and
as the heat intensifies it's also impossible to say exactly
what anything means. It's as if a maths problem in which
two unknowns must be resolved into a third equally unknown
is keeping me awake throughout the day, while
at the same time and almost imperceptibly one is growing
into the enjoyment of seeming transitory pleasures. Oh! July!
(Oh! Over-use of! exclamation marks, but I am so passionate!)
Well come (sic) to summer of choices puzzles
labyrinths and you are lost, aren't you? My private
conundrum, creatures who seem incomplete or who have
refined duplicity to an art, half-human half-beast.
And yes, it is it is, and it's so difficult to choose
between you and August, for you are almost identical,
(twin hearts, burnings, yearnings, and the rhyming turnings)
or would be if September were not such a sultry siren

beguiling me with her undertow and secret wishes. No!
Or shall we fall from here with grace and into
yon icy cauldron? Grey elephant lumbering across the horizon
trying hard to understand and unravel misunderstandings:
you are the September of late summer and early autumn
and wavering of belief. Only with the arrival
(imagine an ocean liner pulling into a parking bay
outside the new shopping mall) of

October and its unfeeling certainties does transparency
finally condescend to bully me with its presence. I am
reminded of how I once fell to my knees to
await a blessing and awoke to see my mother
hanging over me all but obscured by a thick fog. Then
all at once as if time were only a figment or
a fragment of imagination it's December, or January,
or February – it's so impossible to tell the difference
between one enemy and another. They approach
with berets and boots, whispering of swimsuits
and battledress, underwear and promises,
birds in the trees awaiting the thaw. Oh,
but I see nothing has been explained at all, that what
was supposed to be an explanation or
at the very least a description of
how I watch a year go by
has refused to obey the unwritten rules of the form
as well as the written, has not considered
the expectations of those who, attracted by the prospect
of hearing how I watch a year go by, stopped by
to see what I had to say and have now
probably gone home in a huff (a vehicle often taken
by those bearing if not ill-will at least
a modicum of disappointment). But to explain
~~has~~ was never my intention, nor was it my intention
to describe how I watch a year go by. I am sat

at my desk on a cheap chair of the style described
in furniture catalogues as an office chair bought from a shop
not far from here in Tangjiawan (Chinese: 唐家湾)
and on the couch behind me and across the room
Li Min is sat cross-legged with her head in a book
(not literally, that would be uncomfortable; it's a figure of
speech, in the same way as one says, for instance,
I could eat a horse, or my feet are killing me)
and three days ago an idea flittered into what I call
my mind, and it was to write about a year going by,
month after month, somewhat reminiscent
of a shepherd's calendar but in truth
nothing like a shepherd's calendar at all, there are no
sheep here, rather mosquitoes and cockroaches,

but that doesn't matter, it doesn't, for an idea flittering
is only a seed, and one is reminded of Spring,
refreshment of the earth, and Chaucer,
whan that Aprill with his shoures soote
the droghte of March hath perced to the roote,
and bathed every veyne in swich licour
of which vertu engendred is the flour;
whan Zephirus eek with his sweete breeth
inspired hath in every holt and heeth
the tendre croppes, and the yonge sonne
hath in the Ram his half cours yronne, and then to
Summer, and John Ashbery, and no one really knows
or cares whether this is the whole of which parts
were vouchsafed--once--but to be ambling on's
the tradition more than the safekeeping of it. This mulch for
play keeps them interested and busy while the big,
vaguer stuff can decide what it wants--what maps, what
model cities, how much waste space. Life, our
life anyway, is between. We don't mind
or notice any more that the sky *is* green, a parrot
one, but have our earnest where it chances on us,
disingenuous, intrigued, inviting more,
always invoking the echo, a summer's day. And then we arrive
at Autumn, and a predictable but nonetheless Keatsian Keats,
and barred clouds bloom the soft-dying day,
and touch the stubble-plains with rosy hue;
then in a wailful choir the small gnats mourn
among the river sallows, borne aloft
or sinking as the light wind lives or dies;
and full-grown lambs loud bleat from hilly bourn;
hedge-crickets sing; and now with treble soft
the red-breast whistles from a garden-croft;
and gathering swallows twitter in the skies
until Winter arrives, but our Winter is
Frank O'Hara and a city Winter, for we today are posing as
city folk, and understanding the boredom of the clerks
fatigue shifting like dunes within their eyes
a frightful nausea gumming up the works
that once was thought aggression in disguise.
Do you remember? I remember but choose
to feign forgetfulness, and I choose the girl before the gang,

I choose the year and not the life,
I choose the hearth over the party,
I choose the month and not the year,
I choose the discordant before the melodic,
I choose the week ahead of the month,
I choose the ambiguous rather than the debatable,
I choose the day and not the week,
I choose the puzzle rather than the solution,
I choose the silence over the babble,
I choose the present and not the past,
I choose the pleasures of peace, oh Kenneth Koch! and
I choose the surrender unto love – not the resistance.

JOE THE MEEK

I've put the shelf back up and repaired the wall. I leave you
to put the ornaments back in place and re-hang the pictures –
those that are still in one piece. I'll be here on Saturday morning

as usual. Please have the kids ready. I sign myself "The DIY Man".
I have no idea where you are. Perhaps you are on Faraway Island
or on top of Cloud-Hidden Mountain. I hope you are not

down Deep Dark Hole. It's not nice down there. But when you return
(you will return, right?) could you at least message me
so I know I'm not talking to myself? I'll be here on Saturday morning

as usual. Please have the kids ready. I sign myself
                         "Global Repositioning System".
By the way, did you come across my Alexis Zoumbas CD
while you were having your clear-out? I know you

weren't a fan but I kind of miss him. His playing
really annoyed the neighbours, and that was all the inspiration
someone like me needs. I'll be here on Saturday morning

as usual. Please have the kids ready. I sign myself "The Fiddler".
Dearest, did you ever like my mind? I had been thinking
of leaving it to you when I check out in exchange for

occasional touches of your most intimate clothing but this may now be
the all-time mootest of moot points. I am becoming
a connoisseur of the pointless. I'll be here on Saturday morning

as usual. Please have the kids ready. I sign myself "Joe the Meek".
On the turntable as I write this Malcolm and The Countdowns are
spinning out of control, Malcolm's heart having been stolen away

by a post-war party girl. Notice how he doesn't say
his heart's been ripped from his chest. I'll be here on Saturday morning
as usual, so please have the kids ready.

LETTERS FROM THE LIGHT TO THE DARKNESS

Dear The Day,

I wish you were more handsome.
Some say you are charming
but I can't see it: charm,
as far as I know, is more than
possessing the ability to act the part
others expect. Also I do not care
for the way you come and go.
The next time you go, please stay gone.

Yours in the shape of a becoming dishevelment,

"The Fear of Dawn"

*

Dear Social Secretary,

No,
I won't be joining y'all
for supper this evening. Do I strike you as
the kind of person who likes diseases?

Yours in the shape of impending misfortune,

"The Euphemism"

Dear Arranger of Flowers,

Do you not realize
that to place the crocii behind
the lilies is akin to placing
the minnow behind the whale for
the school photograph? But
of course I bow (as do we all) to your long
years in the world of flora and fawning.
There is (it says in your publicity material,
and in the transcript of your divorce proceedings)
nobody else living within range of
an intoxicating perfume who knows more
about where one beauty should stand
in relation to another.

Yours in the shape of several futile liaisons,

"The Lost Cause"

*

Dear Student of Mysteries,

You will find the answers
to every question in
a bottle or three of wine.
Do not always expect clarity,
only more confusion and little comfort.
But do expect warmth and companionship.
Drinking with an intimate friend is
more rewarding than drinking alone,
but drinking alone has its compensations
(and also its condemnations).
I speak of that which I have learned.
If you ever visit my humble dwelling
I will show you my scars.

Yours in the shape of sediment accumulating,

"The Advice Shop"

Dear Hope Springs Eternal,

I heard a very funny joke yesterday
but it loses quite a lot of
its humour in translation.
In fact it loses
all its humour in translation
so I'm not going to tell you it.
Instead, let's go together and gaze at
the sea in all its murky polluted majesty.
We can also watch the aeroplanes coming in
to land. Life is out there somewhere.

Yours in the shape of an all-purpose plastic container,

"The Microscopic Boy"

*

Dear Loiterer,

I have also loitered in vacant hours
and befriended boredom. And I have waited,
and know how pain feels as it evolves
and becomes despair. On the other hand,
I have welcomed the unexpected arrival of
the pantomime horse, and enjoyed
many very funny moments in its company.
Often I have laughed until I thought
my bones would break.

Yours in the shape of a pile of sticks,

"The Lingering Doubt"

Dear May Flower,

It's not unusual
for confusion to follow confession,
for despair to follow delight,
or for turtles to turn out to be tortoises.
The pants, if that is what they are, leave me
breathless. And in a rather self-conscious non sequitur,
the mountain one is now now faced with has
all the characteristics of the lunar landscape.

Yours in the shape of feigned merriment,

"The Turn of the Tide"

*

Dear Under-Achiever,

Try harder! (Fortune is not your Mistress.)

Yours in the shape of success on stilts,

"The Irony Monger"

*

Dear Akela,

It appears we are at odds
about the meaning of discipline.
From my point of view,
the aim of discipline is to ensure
a few moments of self-interested
pleasure during our sojourn in
this vale of toil and tears. It would appear
we have read different books on the subject,
and we have certainly seen different films.
How one can live a life
limited by such archaic strictures
beats me like a gale beats
the mind of an imbecile into nothing
as much as a bag of feathers.

Yours in the shape of an ill wind blows all the time around here,

"The Palm of the Hand"

*

Dear Physician,

Were I able to accurately describe my symptoms
I would be as the scribe in the time of
King Theobald the Rapidly Balding
who so perfectly wrote of the chill winds
blowing through the hollows of his bones
the King had him stuffed and put on display
outside the royal palace before he died.
All I can say is that the chill winds
that blow through my hollows
you would not want them
anywhere near your house,
never mind your body. What I need is
a placebo so I can continue to fool myself
rather than admit to my true condition.

Yours in the shape of misplaced optimism,

"The Lethargy"

Dear Mr. Genius,

Sometimes it seems as if in writing
to you I am writing to myself, but in
the absence of any replies I shall have to
let that pass. Once, when riding in the back of the cart
on the way to market with my mother and Aunt Joan,
I was admonished for telling myself
a story to pass the time. It was then I first felt a feeling
since felt on numberless occasions:
a sense of injustice
at being upbraided for entertaining myself
when nobody else was offering to do it for me.
I have had to be strong; it has not always been easy.

Yours in the shape of confidence ebbing,

"The Seed of Doubt"

*

Dear Emptiness,

I have heard it said
when you pay a call it's impossible to know
if your stay will be brief or stretch
to the end of one's days. My home is
a humble one, and the rooms are already filled with
solitude, so perhaps you could stay with
my sister instead. She is more deserving,
and has a bigger house..

Yours in the shape of trembling hands,

"The Evicted Tenant"

*

Dear Supplier of Dreams,

You draw me to you as a magnet draws base metal.
You entrance, hypnotize, enthrall and petrify me.
In your presence I am as a stone cast into a quarry,
a pebble lost on the beach,
a dust mote in the eye of a hurricane,
and a snowflake in a blizzard.
You take my breath away
as a flaming sheep stuns the ancient shepherd
on the hill of his forefathers.
You leave me speechless
as the glorious angel leaves two sisters
gaping open-mouthed and dumb
at the entrance to a garden of eternally sleeping brothers.
I would write my feelings down
so that my children should know of your dangerous charms
ere they come of age,
but I can't find the words.

Yours in the shape of expected malaise,

"The Theoretician"

*

Dear The Night,

I wish you were taller.
And I notice today
my shadow is thinner
than it has been of late.

Yours in the shape of one's own image,

"The Bed Man"

MAPS AND PLANS

Maps need to be the right way up. A book called
The World Turned Upside Down turned out to be about
not what I expected. Do not predict. Maps are to know.

Maps of sleep. He in her clothes, she in snow. Water
may dissolve a map but not what is mapped. To be pored
over. We are in our positions. Maps of places to go.

Maps are not plans. If they were plans they would be
called plans. Or plans would be called maps. Take
the road south. It will be downhill. Maps are to trust.

Maps of necessity. Turn right at the Yellow River.
Go find the Queen of the Fish. I am a Mermaid. You
are King of the Waters. Maps are to help us navigate.

MAY YOU UNFURL

May you turn into the flesh-covered protagonist of myth. May you illuminate the scene in all your fire.

If the manager of the local supermarket has his way you may soon be moving rubbish from one location to another.

May you turn the eyes of monsters into gems of the most serene. May you envelope our remaining days in your dreamy wonder.

If the manager of the local supermarket has his way you may soon be filling his shelves.

May you turn one corner into a lagoon of dragonflies and another into the welcoming softness of a platoon of lambs. May you never fear.

If the manager of the local supermarket has his way you may soon be making tea and doing some photocopying.

May you turn the page and discover solace in the shade of an ageing almond tree. May you discover hope refusing to be abandoned after having abandoned hope.

If the manager of the local supermarket has his way you may soon be crawling from the night shift and stealing home with sores and hurts.

May you turn down the offer of boundless ice. May you accept the challenge of stars blanketing an endless heaven.

If the manager of the local supermarket has his way you may soon be watching it rain into the shutters and darkness falling upon the bleach mills.

May you unfurl like the thunder as it slams into the window. May your heart come to rest in my eyes and flower even as we fade into one another.

MEET THE POET

What began as a tear-stained conversation over a pint of ale
turned into a popular television sitcom
beloved by millions
but the authors (having given up their day-jobs) preferred to see it

as a tragedy of Grecian proportions -- but they should have known
our writings, our precious children, are often misunderstood.
It's, you know, wrong to castigate anyone
for chuckling

during the opening chapters of *Moby Dick*. And *The Scarlet Letter*
is now seen not so much as a futile attempt to assuage
Puritan guilt as one of the finest tools ever devised
for the filling of student lives

with misery, something with which we may safely assume
Nathaniel Hawthorne would not have had much sympathy.
We shall never know for sure, but to be honest we
don't care a hell of a lot. Poets

are among the most unsympathetic of folk
and often fail to understand themselves, yet it has ever been
the lot of the versifier to be hailed by the tribe
as head cook, philosopher,

Jack-of-All-Trades and bottle-washer
by the jury of his or her peers,
and someone to turn to in times of distress and/or boredom.
So it was that last night

came a-knocking at my door
the mayor and his deputies and the ladies of the Knitting Guild.
When I answered their knock
I was wearing my

"My girlfriend says she loves me but she lets me go out
wearing this t-shirt" t-shirt
because I have a sense of humour. The mayor on his knees
begged me

to write a poem so the ne'er-do-wells
who own the town's hot-shot-night-spots and low-life-wallow-dives
might gather up their shady belongings and
high-tail it away

so the ladies might not be hampered in their endeavours
to clean up the community and get everyone
knitting their way to Heaven.
Well, it behoved me

to clarify my position concerning morality.
The local good time gals are of variable quality, I said.
My ambition is to retire from poetry and start a Hellfire Club.
I like recreational sex and video games.

And eating. Apropos of which, I once fell asleep between courses
at my third-favourite restaurant — The Muses,
a name that almost stops me from eating there. It's only
the waitresses and the bread and butter pudding

that keep me going back. I noticed when
the mayor and his deputies and the ladies of the Knitting Guild
turned their collective back on me as if they could not
get away fast enough

how at that time of the evening
if one looks long and very hard into the sky
there are words hanging, waiting to be plucked like stars
from space. The words

I harvested that night were (let me check my journal;
oh yeah:) credulous, fraternize, dyspepsia, tape,
Uzbekistan, dowager, plead, bind, syrup, and one short phrase:
"Be ever moved by life."

MONTAIGNE

Because I've agreed to go downtown
and shop for cosmetics she can't buy
in the stores where she lives it will be
as if, although I'm consigned to the junk,
we are somehow still together.

As I write this I am eating bread
and cheese, and several thoughts
are crossing my mind. Back and forth
they go, like chickens in the snow.
(In Montaigne I have read of how
Francis Bacon died of a chill caught
when stuffing a chicken full of snow,
and last night in the chilly capital
arriving from my sub-tropical home
the sudden drop in temperature
caught me out too. I now have what
my mother used to call "the sniffles".)

Speaking of Montaigne, I have also read
in him an opinion, how no one would buy
a horse without first taking off the saddle
and bridle, and similar considerations
should apply in marriage, which was
why before agreeing to anything I insisted
we see one another naked. That was
when our country was another country,
and the fashion of kissing girls was
much to my taste. I almost wore out my lips.

This evening in the murky light
I misread "his book" for "he took" but frankly
my mind was not really on the job in hand.
I was thinking of buying cosmetics
for a face I can't touch. Lips I can't kiss.

NOTES FOR A LETTER

proceeding from Coleridge

1. If the weatherman is right then this period of calm will not last the night. There is a new moon and rain and wind is coming.

2. A love loved and not returned. Spring, a season that dies.

3. In the presence of this beauty there is only seeing. Not feeling.

4. The world cannot stir the smothered heart. Still are the fountains that are the life.

5. Always the glorious sky and a maiden quietly raising her quiet eyes.

6. Ten thousand friends. (So modern!) It's alright then, seated upon a stone of the imagination.

7. Prayer eyes.

8. Remembrance (1): the play of an eyelash upon a cheek. Happiness.

9. How to bruise a soul.

10. Remembrance (2): sorrow and pain sent from afar. Happiness's opposite.

11. In absence the mind wanders, enjoying joy and morbid in its occasional sadness. Or is it the other way around?

12. cf. The Happiness Business. (A tree in blossom, a branch withering.)

13. To be the comforter! To be the healer! To share both delight and pains! To have such a hope.

14. The wind moans now like a lost child.

15. And as the wind rages may sleep cover you gently.

16. A rough path is no stranger. But the imagination: whatever happened to that? Smothered by dreams.

17. In abstractions begin the distractions that become Nature. This is now Temper.

18. There is a bird, the nightingale, that sings love songs while a thorn pricks its breast. There is a happiness that doubles misery.

19. The things that once were are no longer. Briefly, this is how it stands.

20. Light has to come from within. That is joy. We have named what we have lost.

ON DEATH

(slightly extracted from Montaigne)

To philosophize or so I read is to prepare for death
And thinking about it as the black and white bird alights
On the balcony to feed on the peanuts placed there
Especially for him and his friends it occurs to us that
We once were of the mind that pleasure was our target
In life or what passes for life in the modern age but
An argument might be had even between romancers
Over what constitutes pleasure for it says here
The pleasures of the mind and the body are different
Which perhaps needs elucidating but this is not the place
And the black and white bird is flown away and now
The less flamboyant but more numerous wagtails are
Arrived to take their share as the afternoon sun
Bathes in unseasonable warmth our little patch of world
Where it would appear to be a truism that the end
Of our course is death which is not a cheerful thought
To be concerned with but some philosophers would say
It is not death we fear as much as the lead up to it
For death is only a momentary and passing event whereas
The run-up can last a literally agonizing long time
Unless one is for example lucky enough to die
Between a woman's thighs like Pope Clement V
But even that would not be a happy way to go for some
For let's face it the world is brimming with people
Who would not wish to be found in that position
And as we gaze out across this undeniably pleasant vista
Somewhere a horse stumbles and a tile falls from a roof
The rider falls and rises no more the pedestrian does not
Know and never will know what hit him and consider now
Are you prepared for that which when our blossoming youth
Rejoiced in spring never troubled our careless minds at all.

ONE MORE SIP

Oh, one more sip and I'll be done.

Dear Samantha, if that's your name, are you as much of a bookworm as I? The inquisitors have expressed surprise at the similarity of our answers, but how could they understand two minds working as if, not so much in parallel but, to be more exact, in tandem. Which reminds me, I did not learn to ride a bicycle until I was 28 years old.

Please don't tell anyone all the things you know about me.

One more sip and I'll be done.

Dear Samantha, if I am not talking to myself, are you the fingers wrapped around the body of the snake or the stone at the heart of the stone? I'm worried because your hair is falling out. Or is it mine? Yesterday I tumbled from the quayside into the harbour and was only saved by the helping hand of the idiot boy, and in the nick of time! I cannot swim, nor can I tell the difference between sarcasm and out-and-out cruelty.

Please, please don't tell anyone all the things you know about me.

Oh, one more sip and I'll be done.

Dear Samantha, if you even exist, are you wondering how come I have been chosen to be The Chosen One? Well, when asked, 85% of customers surveyed said they would recommend me to a friend. Because of this, and because I have the coy personality of a coy lamb, I have been earmarked in spite of my spending way too much time in a world of my own.

Anyway, please don't tell anyone all the things you know about me.

ONE OF THE SADDEST YEARS

A library full of books
and a gallery filled with pictures
and a mausoleum full of worthies
and the less than worthy
and a park with the grand gesture of fountains
and the grass under foot as we walk
side by side murmuring about how
although this has been one of the saddest years
urbanity and geniality
are what distinguish us from our peers.

The mists of winter obscure the outbuildings
and the outbuildings block our view of the hills
and the hills come between us and the ocean
and the ocean distances us
from people we love. And on arriving home
we find everything is covered in a fine film of dust
and much of the dust is patterned
by the boot-prints of tiny creatures
who have danced in our absence,
and we wish we had been at that frolic.

PERMANENCE

Nothing's realistic, especially reality,
so as the winged pig pokes its head out
of the corrugated cardboard crate you keep it in
and takes a look around at the junked vans
by the side of the junked river
and asks in its winsome yet whining way
how come there ain't no sunshine since you been gone baby
the assumption is that words of wisdom may yet fall
out of the tree we planted a hundred years ago
but what worries me is the way in which
nothing seems to be quite as it used to be. For example,

in the good old days a dreadful monster called Beowulf lived in the sea
and came up out of the sea and ate everybody it bumped into at the mall
until Robin Hood came along and gave it some chewing gum and it choked
because it wasn't used to chewing it always simply swallowed whole

and in other old days when men wore armour to keep brains and balls safe
chain mail was delivered twice a day but just once on Sundays
they cut down endless mountains to build those impregnable aqueducts
and invented the gentle art of jousting because chess is rather boring

then in yet another history time when Queen George the Innumerable
ruled over United Britain in the time of The Age Of Irrationality
the theatre such as it was was full of sex and violence and popcorn
and it wasn't safe to go out on the street either before or after dark

and there are endless examples like these, demonstrating how
things changed between the time we decided which boat to catch
and when we drove out to the harbour in our donkey cart.
And I know what you're thinking. I know what you're going to say.

That I broke the solemn oath sworn upon the sacred stone so long ago.
That I abandoned you to the Fates.
That when you woke up this morning the Bird of Bounty
I brought home yesterday evening had turned into an oaken chest

within which ancient documents proved I was not of an old family
but only recently cobbled together out of bits of string, wire
and old batteries. Eyes of glass from broken bottles.

Come on. Catch up.
You can find my autobiography online if you look hard enough.
And history is written by the people who win.
Who's writing this?

RENDEZVOUS

At the bus stop in front of the mall
but there might be too many people there
it's not a very good place to meet we might miss each other
but it's easy to find the 69 bus runs every 13 minutes
the first one being at 06.36 or 06.41 on Sundays
and the 10A is every 16 minutes the first one is 06.25
seven days a week but it goes the long way round.

Outside the library if it's not raining I'll be
holding *The Consolation of Philosophy* I've read it four times
now I'm on my fifth Boethius was in prison when he wrote it
in AD 524 mine is the Penguin edition it cost 30 yuan.

In Starbucks I'll try and get a couch
but it's not always possible if I don't get
a couch I'll be I don't know where I'll be how could I
know Starbucks now has more than 750 stores
in the People's Republic of China two years ago there
were none in this city now we have three.

The lobby of the White House Hotel you don't need to
be a guest to go inside a room there costs
from around 800 yuan and up but it's cheaper
if you book online there's a site I use all the time it's good
although I don't trust the hotel reviews unless
I write them myself which sometimes I have done.

Round the back of the Zhu Ying supermarket
where they stack used cardboard from boxes
stuff comes in nobody goes round there in the evening
it's dark the girls especially steer clear but it's too near the bins
I saw a family of rats there last time it was a family of five
one rat for each bin they were very well organized.

At the entrance to the cemetery a resting place for
at the last count 972 souls partaking of glory.

SINCE YOUR RETURN I'VE BEEN WAITING FOR YOU
TO LEAVE AGAIN

Dear Consuela,

Since your return I am a stranger to myself. I look at my reflection on the bottom of my tobacco tin and see not the Prince I was expecting but an old man who looks like he might be a gardener from a faraway estate.

Dear Bella,

Since your return you have been so lively. How you do hop about! I have always been an admirer of tranquillity. I account for it by a general lack of energy and enthusiasm for life. Calm is my favoured condition.

Dear Pandora,

Since your return everything is different. My skin, for instance. I don't think it has ever been so velvety.

Dear Melancholia,

Since your return even the famous John's pudding people of poetic legend are refusing to come out and play. I loathe having to make up my own solitary entertainments, but so be it.

Dear Atahuallpa,

Since your return you have been banging on about the song Marc wrote for you, but that was 1968 and the past is the past, and is the present only in our imaginations. Don't frown.

Dear Delilah,

Since your return I'm without everything of value.

Dear Paranoia,

Since your return it has been too daunting to enter the forest. There is nothing but darkness among the trees, and if the sunlight will not go in among them I don't see why I should. I am not braver than the Sun.

Dear Sylvia,

Since your return it has been nothing but romantic chatter but it's pretty much all just noise. The more we use them the more our words lose any meaning they had.

Dear Fortuna,

Since your return the donkey at the mill has been restless. Perhaps his sense of distrust is heightened by your presence. He pulls with all his might and turns the wheel but the look in his eyes seems to suggest he knows it is all for nothing.

Dear Anaesthesia,

Since your return you will not be surprised to hear I feel nothing.

SNOW FALLING

The first snow has fallen, is falling.
Some people have never seen snow. It is
their loss. But I assume they can get it
on the internet if they can be bothered.

It's possible to imagine snow, but impossible
to imagine it correctly. In the same way
it's impossible to imagine correctly
how another person feels
as they pass from the heaven of their sky
to a normal day, a normal life,
a normal passing. Nobody has felt
what I feel, nobody has felt what you feel.
Snow is falling, and it is your own snow.

And in this small world, real
or imagined, other fallings fall and drift
down and away, out of sight and beyond touch.
The blue moment drops out of the clouds
(insert simile, if you wish)
and then, catching an updraft, takes wing
momentarily, but falls again, tired
and helpless under its own weight
although it weighs almost nothing
being composed only of light and love. In
a moment of unforeseen sadness the crown
of the King of Happiness topples off the head
of the King of Happiness, and being made of
but smiling serenity it too is taken by the air
and translated from one world to another.
It's impossible to imagine correctly
how different this world is from that other,
as impossible as imagining
your lips approaching mine.

And attempts have been made to rescue
the drifting and the lost. Hempen rope, magnet,
rod and line, butterfly net, naked willpower –

all as fruitless as an apple tree in winter
(a simile as hopeless as the hopelessness
it aims to represent). Imagine trying to pin
an idea to a cloud: it's like imagining
a belief in a dream coming true.

The snow is still falling. By morning
it will have covered the darkness and
started in on obliterating the daylight.
I hear some people have never experienced
anything like it, anything like
all you love being reduced to a memory.
There has been loss
and there always will be. And one day
the earth and the sky will go away.
Imagine reaching out a hand and being unable
to stop them leaving. It's impossible
to imagine it correctly, but it's possible
to imagine it wrongly and feel the snow
as it settles around your ankles
and gradually becomes deeper and deeper.

SPLOSH

Well, first we had some splosh
then we had some more. Before
long the stars in the heavens were
on fire. The horizon was lined with
dancing girls the shape of trees or
the other way around. For a moment
I thought I'd lost my glasses but then
realized I was wearing them. When
the splosh was gone we fell asleep
one by one by one in a neat heap
somewhat resembling firewood.

Well, come dawn the snow showed
signs of wear and tear. The orphans
were standing around kicking
their heels waiting for the bus
to take them to the seaside. It was
the day of the outing. Sand dunes
shift and shimmy as wind blows. I'd
thought it too cold to go to the seaside
but one look at those awful children
and I knew I was probably wrong.

Well, the day was one moment
sun and the next snow-laden cloud. After
lunch I put on my shoes to go walking
and the rain duly fell. I was not in
the best of moods: the news from the
world I'd seen at breakfast had been
terribly downing, and there was
not enough milk for my Corn Flakes.
I went out but not for very long.

Well, in the evening we craved
splosh but there was none
and no-one had any money so we
looked at the television for a couple of
hours. Nobody could be bothered to turn

it on so burdensome was the ennui
of our minds, what with being awake
and all. Before I climbed wooden hill
I looked out the window to check
on the mountains. They were looming
but somehow somewhat reassuring.

Well, months followed months
as moths follow moths
and eventually we arrived at the autumn of life
and the music we loved caused leaves
to fall off trees for it comprised
the melodies of our falling. We posted
signs around the homestead saying
Keep up.
If you don't follow this you'll get lost.
In honour of our travels
I translated them:
脑子转得快一点.
如果你不紧跟我的思路, 最后你会不知道我在说什么.

Well, what does it add up to? I go
to the supermarket and get some
cheap splosh and feel a lot better
but the feeling doesn't last. I've noticed
how feelings when you look back
at them have a terrifying habit of not
lasting. And you look in the glass
and there it languishes: your life,
and it's kind of really mystifying.

THE AUTHOR'S PREFACE TO THE READER

Sitting once in a very studious posture
and henceforth falling into the clutches of melancholy
I assumed the role of concubine to the empress. How many hours
went by until the pigeons left the roof of the den I cannot tell
but procrastinating ill becomes me as it transpires
so let's get on and get this over with.

With my paper before me
I began composition of a song to be uttered in perfect solitude
at times of extreme distress. But distress in the world must be
leavened by humour, to which end a buffoon enters stage right
carrying with some difficulty a baby elephant which then explodes,
covering rows A to F in blood and guts and umbrella stands.

My pen in my ear
seems to have caused a slight infection which in turn
has led to 85 per cent deafness on that side. When Penelope comes
into the story in Act XIV Scene VIII her diatribe is unreliable
because I couldn't hear clearly but the general drift is pretty clear:
she's pissed off about what happened to the bag of sparrows.

My elbow on the table
would not be surprising but the absence of arm is alarming. Every
artist has an intention concealed somewhere about their person
and in this half-light it will take you a more than usually long time
to find mine. Issues that confront the ordinary person
are no concern of your author, which is a clue.

And my cheek on my hand
reminds me at the end of life of my hand on Penelope's cheek
under the drooping eaves of the drying house. Always
the sound of workmen working disturbs the quiet hours I needed
to write down what I thought about everything
so perhaps what I offer you now is ill-considered and imperfect.

The man often says the wrong thing.
The idiot often says the wrong thing.
Do the algebra. Meanwhile,
as if believing the albatross is not a bird of prey,
the pastured horse gazes upward
toward reflections of sea. Sunset's beautiful
and the smoke from cigars intoxicating. Having
cast my vote I open the book at random,
and on page 2307 (4 being my lucky number)
are these words, and only these words:
"You are fortunate to be here."
I recommend *The Book of Lies*
if you can find it cheap on Amazon, or
steal it from the school library.

Here are some more quotations:
"The invisible maiden is not trustworthy."
"The sixpence ceased to be legal tender on 1st July 1993."
"The mandarin is a musical instrument of the lute family."
"The albatross is a distant relation of the pigeon."
"The transparent maiden blocks the view."
"This is a free country."
"The sonnet is a young swan."
"The florin was legal tender until 30th June 1980."
"The temperatures in temperate countries are generally
relatively moderate, rather than extreme hot or cold."
"The opaque maiden's purpose is crystal clear."
"More quotations can be found later in this poem."

I close the book as if there's something better to do
and mount the bicycle I long to become. "Bay of Pigs (Detail)"
is on the iPod and sunset's beautiful
tonight and the next few evenings.
Aircraft disappear behind pink clouds; later
I will cut my finger while preparing supper.
My disinterestedness in social issues
is impossible to conceal but
the sky has my full support most of the time.

I gaze upward toward it and then down
upon and into pavilions of dance. Horses
possess a refreshing wisdom but not many people know
or care. When I report for work tomorrow
it will be as if a dream is ending
and beginning over again.
Over again. Oh, I do so love to paint ceilings
brimming with gamboling horses
gamboling across a field filled with fellows
wearing fedoras and other items
beginning with the letter F:
fish-net stockings, full-bodied frocks,
fine-mesh vests, and four dollar collars.

By the bye,
I'm hungry - but from here to the refrigerator
is a long way. Once upon a time
(before records began) (people sang to one another)
I remember setting out for the polling booths
and not arriving. It was encouraging,
but *The Book of Lies* puts everything
into its proper perspective:

"The albatross was once the cage bird of choice in fashionable society,
but as the repetitious nature of politics came increasingly to bore the
pants off people the red-cheeked canary began to gain favour. Its
being much cheaper to feed was a point in its favour in times of
economic downturn. Thus is the dictum that necessity is the mother
of intention proven."

THE DROWNER

1. (Drafts)

As one pushed off the end of a pier who pauses
to reflect how it's so tiring to wash your hair
and wishes there were a handmaiden nearby
to whom he could say "Come wash my hair for me.
Here, use the water from this convenient ocean."
and the handmaiden with her hands and her servility
would do his bidding for she is unreal and kind –

As one thrown overboard from a skiff who remembers
how in moments of the greatest distress
trivialities will sometimes push themselves to the fore
and he wonders if there is a beauty parlour nearby
("I have heard such good things about *Nails & Nails*")
for his concerns and regrets are not for wife and child,
house and garden, car and motor home, joint account
and mortgage burden, scripture and faith,
philosopher's stone and crystal talisman but for
broken fingernail, unsightly nose hair –

As one left for dead in the wake of his hijacked yacht
who sees the mermaid swimming at his side
and she in reply to his "You are beautiful and impossible;
take me in your arms and save my life" says
"I bet you wish you'd taken those swimming lessons
you always thought about but never got around to"
then dives below the surface never to be seen again
until he wakes up in the shade of desert island palms
and looks blearily into the eyes of the dusky maiden
who mops his brow as her tears become pearls –

2. (A fragment)

Until the day I was keelhauled at the admiral's command I did not know
what to be keelhauled meant, being new to the ocean and more of a
philosopher who had spent many hours pondering the relative qualities

of the concrete and the abstract, of water and land, of air and the opposite of air (which I had been attempting to name) than a sailor married to the sea having been born of water and thus destined to dissolve at the end of his time. How I came to be at sea is an anecdote worth the telling. It all began one day on the pier at Brighton, and I was disputing with a fellow thinker (he calls himself a thinker but I dispute

3. (all that was found of *The Last Will and Testament*)

and to Romance my heart
and to Desire my loins
and to Hope my eyes
and to Faith my intellect
and to Trust my bones
and to Endeavour my breath
and to Courage my blood
and to Perseverance my afterlife

4. (*The Last Will and Testament* in context)

He was in the last drawer they opened. Everyone was surprised at how much he had shrunk. They knew he had withdrawn into himself in his later years but finding him to be no larger than a moderately-sized vibrator was a shock to them all, especially since with his shaved head he looked like one too.

Clasped in his left hand was a scrap of paper on which could be discerned a miniscule script which, with the aid of a magnifying glass, proved to be the words presented here as all that was found of *The Last Will and Testament*.

What had become of the rest of the will is impossible to say, although the consensus seems to be he was eating the paper at the time of his death: the frayed edges suggest small nibbles had been taken from it.

One person (we shall keep his identity concealed for now) has suggested the document was not a will but a poem. But as more than one person has said, just because what remains looks like a bit of a poem doesn't mean it *was* a bit of a poem.

THE ELEMENTS

1.

As he wiped the dust from the ancient Imperial 70 typewriter
He tried his very best to remember
The great idea that had come to him last night
Moments before he fell asleep.

2.

Be not always the great he or she. Your faults
(Inelegance, shame, burglary, unnecessary tourism,
Forgetfulness, vacancy & sincerity) are minor.
Some may find this all too wide-eyed.
In the great world the biggest thing that has happened recently
Is that the great world doesn't seem to care about you at all.
But a new love affair is glowing upon your brow now.

3.

Because we long for the opportunity to go out
We do not want the rain to last forever.
We long for a chance to show off our new sunwear
& for all we know our moment in the Sun may be fleeting.

4.

Breathing at the Sun is okay.
Breathing on the Sun is not okay.
Breathing because of the Sun is poetic.

5.

Discretion has never been an option
& a list of options that are no longer options is a dead end with me.
Please take this bouquet of roses
Before my arms drop off.

6.

I went to the store to get beans
Because I like beans:
It doesn't matter to me how Pythagoras said
To abstain from beans; Pythagoras also said
Not to step over a crossbar, & I'm always
Stepping over crossbars, it's something I enjoy.
I also let swallows share my roof,
& I'm always plucking garlands.
I'm famous for plucking garlands.

7.

I'm not sure about anything definite now.
The line between sea & sky is too far off
& beyond any use I could ever make of it. Seriously,
Is this what folk do?
Blink & everything's shifted.

8.

In sleep something takes shape & I rather admire the shape.
Don't tell me to talk about the real world when this is all the world.
I am writing my complete life story
Before I die by drowning, or so I seem to wish to say.
Perhaps there is a big mistake being made
But my eyes are wide open & I can't see it.
We are being examined, always examined.

9.

Life can surely spring no surprises now.
A sacrifice has been demanded by people in the know
So perhaps it is time to burn the early works.

10.

My head is lost inside this book -
The autobiography of an elephant.
One assumes it was ghost-written.
In some cultures elephants are revered as gods
& in others derided as circus entertainers.

11.

No, I hear myself saying. You're wrong.
I'm a salvationist come to bring you cushion love
& all its redolent splendour,
We make angelic choices against the will
Of the world. & all our panic buttons are undone.

12.

O sparrow, it's time to start singing.
Sunlight drips off the tree branches
& we give thanks
but people think we don't really mean them.

13.

One's manner should strike people as natural, not forced.
Try not to compensate by strained strangeness for lack of pure merit;
This is what unmitigated failures do so try not to behave like one.

14.

So much for civic responsibility:
We could have planted flowers but decided not to.
Instead we took to buffalo ranching.
It did not make us popular with the neighbours.

15.

Thank you for teaching me philosophy.
I owe you some money.
But I was never really sure if you were actually there.
Nor me neither.
So many times have I been mislaid.
I wander lonely.
The only proof we have is pain needs to exist
& loss is everything.

16.

The days spent learning music were the happiest of my life.
Things only began to sour when I turned my attention
To composing my "Symphony for Approaching Night".
I don't think it's worth regretting because
Things go sour all the time
& wisdom may be discovered any time & by accident.

17.

The thing above our heads
Is emptying itself upon us.
It feels like we're dissolving.

18.

Then one day the idea hits.
You can change the world.
But it's fifty years too late.

19.

There is a benign life to be written
But there must also be its opposite.
Do not slip into being a glum person,
Your name floating upon the sea breeze
With all the sinking ships, but be your own unusual.
Let folk register an air of mild surprise
On discovering your fears. The lines of life
Are well-known, but whatever you do
Remember that this isn't what happiness is.

20.

There's a weather beacon on the high-rise.
Nothing is to do with emotional outpourings.
This township is under pressure to explode.
I don't know if it will or not. & I don't care.

21.

Waking up next to a mermaid
It occurred to me I could not swim.
Don't fret, she bubbled. I have you.
My heart was at rest but my mind could not be.

22.

We elect to continue in much the same vein
As gold and silver wander through rock
Not going anywhere much -- only waiting.

23.

What you think about when alone should be victory rather than defeat.
In old age aim to be princely, not lordly.
Be generous with time, company and affection.
This afternoon I'm not sure if the sun is not coming out.

24.

When I lived beside the ocean
There was a sense of imminent drowning
But also something of romance.
I miss those days in sight of water -
But of all the waters this has been the worst:
Tears shed for the perfect unattained lover.

THE NEXT TIME YOU WRITE A LIST POEM

1. (Found Poem from Various Sources)

I've forgotten how to play the violin,
how to scrape and abrade
and how from that scraping and abrading
draw moments of beauty and delight
or sadness and longing or
the sound of a cat in its death throes.
And I've forgotten the method you taught me
of retaining essence of rainbow into old age;
this forgetting occurred as the music slowly disappeared
down the drain into the sewers and far out to sea.
I've forgotten how to fly;
my wings are turned to stone.
I've forgotten what to do with all these mirrors.
I've forgotten that dragons are the new unicorns
and serpents are as trustworthy as most men.
I forget what I learned about how to tell the difference
between a kingdom close at hand
and distant realms of the imagination.
I've forgotten all about etiquette and decorum
and who to love and who to stay away from.
I've forgotten so much,
even how to say what one so desperately wants to say,
even what one wants to say.

2. (To a Gentleman Rumoured to be a Horse Thief)

The next time you write a list poem
that sounds like one of my list poems
please put my name at the bottom of it. Thank you.
I think all sources should be acknowledged like
when a river begins to flow and it can't be stopped
like a mouth that can't be closed or an avalanche
that can't be outrun. I know those are bad whatyamacalls
but I'm trying to be original. Sometimes don't you think
mere disgrace is a bad idea and a hot iron on the rump
more a suitable weapon of choice for people
who don't really fit anywhere?

Society somewhat disturbs me and solitude
both enforced and adopted seems these days to be
a more comfortable way of life. There are between
no and two people I can comfortably live with now
and in their absence I have some spare chairs
and room in my bed for impossible imaginary friends.
I know this chunk doesn't really fit here but
there's nowhere else for it to go.

The next time you write a list poem
that sounds as if I wrote it then threw it away
please put a footnote at the bottom of the page
with my name and address and phone number
so people can call me and see if I'm still alive
and not been replaced by a machine. I think
all imitations should be acknowledged and
the only thing stopping me from naming names is
discretion. Sometimes don't you think a new career
would be better than continuing a mere scrivener?
I've often thought that restraint is an undervalued
grace. Anyway, thank you for your time. I know you
are busy with dictionaries and photocopiers and the like.

THINGS MY FATHER NEVER SAID

1.

The dove of love
perches in the most unlikely places.

2.

When tears roll down your cheek
it's a sign you're not mine.

When tears roll down my cheek
you know I'm not myself.

3.

As snowflakes fall at your feet
and condensation freezes on the windowpane;

as the bud blooms into the flower
and the rainbow enraptures a child;

as the shopkeeper slams the door in your face
and the police warn you to keep your distance;

as the gods bless you
and the sun shines on your head;

as men look upon you with disdain
and women can't be bothered even to go that far –

so love has its ups and downs, my son.

4.

There's nothing I don't know
about the pigeon of despair.

5.

Your hair looks good today.

6.

Let's slam on some music
and remind ourselves
why
in the maelstrom of our days
we remember there can be many loves
and it's overwhelming
and I don't believe in God anymore
only the grace of life
so let's go out and get drunk.

TO NIGEL PICKARD

You know as well as I do
it's impossible to write about some things
and adequately express how one feels.
However much we value words
and live for words
we know words fail us at the most important times.

We can get close, but not close enough.

Allow me to be selfish
and say if it goes on like this
there'll be nobody around to say Goodbye
when it's my turn.

And I'll tell you something else:
it took about 15 seconds to write
those 11 lines.
Which proves some kind of point, I think.

But since I was told
I've been walking around numb.
I want to give you one of those poems you love
that crap on for about a page and a half
and you seem to understand them better than I do --
and I *wrote* the fuckers.
Hey,
I'll bring you one when I come, okay?

WHY I AM ALWAYS PEEKING OVER MY SHOULDER

Umbrella complicate of tree-house -
I'm threatened. Girl horror, I didn't see the knife
They called the fictitious luminary I blurry stared into the starry starry light &
in thepassage-way-cum-shelter O unbecoming beauty but never
quite sad enough to be considered an alarming case such circum-
stance and so examined but if and also the bird on bough was fall-
ing into angel's terminus or maybe that was only in a dream and
whether or not rising death rates or falling in love of course we are
not
machines but threatened by annexation and examination O life
expectancy how nature tricks and however it is it is isn't it, a
rhetorical question

3 CLOSURES

1.

and left a note for the cleaning lady to say she didn't have to come and clean any more because a little dirt no longer mattered.

2.

into the distance, and the distance was endless.

3.

and that was the end of that.

Selections From

Dramatic Works

Scenes from FLIRTS IN SKIRTS

Scene 1: the kitchen just behind a chap's left ear.

Bud: What are these?
Jed: They are photographs of girls' knees.
Bud: Where did they come from?
Jed: I took them with my new Canon EOS 100D with an EF 70-200mm f/2.8L USM Telephoto lens
Bud: Don't you know that girls' knees are evil?
Jed: They make me feel like mealtime.
Bud: Girls' knees are the invention of Satan. He went to the bottom of the abyss and scooped up a handful of the blackest evil and compressed it into bone and cartilage to make girls' knees.
Jed: But I am in love with girls' knees.
Bud: You are a clown man.

Scene 4: the inside of a chap's skull, just outside the brain.

Jed: I am in love with Betty.
Bud: She is a flirt. Forget her. She does not believe in God.
Jed: But she has legs, and is always smiling toward my house.
Bud: All girls have legs, except some of the severely disabled.
Jed: But she wears such short skirts, I am in love with them.
Bud: Short skirts are the invention of Satan. He invented them during his clothing period.
Jed: But Betty is my Destiny.
Bud: You are a man idiot.

Scene 11: the balcony of a chap's ear lobe.

Jed: Look at this! It's a holographic Betty for me to play with when the real Betty is somewhere else.

Bud: You have rendered me utterly speechless, but I have to say that the leaps and bounds of modern science are the invention of Satan. The list of abominations modern science has brought into being seems never-ending and in case you don't know includes, in no particular order, glow-in-the-dark dogs, cellphones, thinking shoes, almost anything made of brightly-coloured plastic, and the artificial heart, which I include because it renders the recipient utterly incapable of true romance. Satan is so ridiculously productive it's obvious he never sleeps.

Jed: But holographic Betty is tremendous. She is wearing small and transparent lingerie and stiletto heels and nothing else.

Bud: You are a nonsense man with no sense.

Scene 14: the alleyway behind a chap's eyes.

Bud: You look awfully smart today. Is that a clean t-shirt?

Jed: I am meeting Betty's friend Coco. I want to make a good impression.

Bud: I take it Coco is a girl.

Jed: Betty says she is already mine, all I have to do is show up and she will direct me to her secret love buttons.

Bud: Love buttons are the invention of Satan. He invented them as part of his scheme for making things easy for people without imagination.

Jed: They are genius.

Bud. You are a hollowed man.

Scene 25: the laundry basket next to a fellow's elbow room.

Bud: You called out Betty's name in your sleep last night.
Jed: She is the girl of my dreams.
Bud: Then you called out Lorraine's name.
Jed: She is the girl of my dreams too.
Bud: Then you called out Shirley and Mabel and Doreen and another one that was muffled so I couldn't make it out.
Jed: They are the girls of my dreams, even when they are muffled. Sometimes the muffled ones are the best.
Bud: Dreams are the invention of Satan. He invented them when he found that God had made sleep so we could hide from the darkness of night. And then he put girls into them as an extra dose of evil.
Jed: Well, I never seem able to get enough sleep.
Bud: You are a man exclamation mark.

Scene 29: the window in a fellow's chest.

Bud: You smell bad.
Jed: Betty and Lorraine say that I smell like a wild beast and they love it, so I am never going to wash again.
Bud: You are attracting flies.
Jed: Betty and Lorraine say I have a natural animal attraction and it makes their girlie underwear melt.
Bud: Melting girlie underwear is the invention of Satan. It's another one from his clothing period. He invented it as an alternative to God's flannelette
contraceptives collection.
Jed: It is wonderful, and there is endless variety too.
Bud: You are become man goo.

Scene 36: the cupboard where a fellow keeps his face.

Jed: I can't talk now. I have to text Betty.
Bud: You're always texting Betty.
Jed: It's one of the reasons I have fingers.
Bud: But you said you would harvest some berries for our lunch.
Jed: Betty is my lunch, and all my other meals too. If you saw her spread out on the table you would forget all about berries too.
Bud: Edible girls are the invention of Satan. He invented them when he saw what God had come up with for the cookery competition.
Jed: My mouth waters when I think about Betty.
Bud: I always thought you were a pickle man.

Scene 41: the entrance to a fellow's hair.

Bud: Where are you?
Jed: Over here, in the shadows of Betty and Lorraine.
Bud: It's dangerous in the shadows cast by girls.
Jed: So I have heard, but I don't care.
Bud: The shadows cast by girls are the invention of Satan. He made them out of doom's entrails and stuff from his box of tricks labelled "Tricks With Darkness and Light."
Jed: Well, I am in love with them. They are the shape of Betty and Lorraine.
Bud: But don't you wonder how come there are shadows in the middle of the night?
Jed: The middle of the night is when I love them the most.
Bud: You are a man booby.

Scene 68½: the bathroom under a chap's bed.

Jed: My trousers have acquired a dreadful disease.
Bud: Of a sexually transported nature?
Jed: Of course. I wouldn't have it any other way.
Bud: Well, that's very Elizabethan. Or Romantic. Or even Victorian.
Perhaps it's also Postmodern, come to think of it.
Jed: I transcend historical and aesthetic periods.
Bud: Sexually transported diseases, it goes without saying , are the
invention of Satan. He invented them to put a dash of fear and restraint
into the otherwise fun pastime of coitus.
Jed: At least it's only my trousers.
Bud: For now. It will spread unless you take the appropriate action. I
suppose Betty is to blame.
Jed: It could be Betty. Or Lorraine. Or Coco. Or Beatrice. Or Suki. Or
Chantelle. Or the Anderson twins.
Bud: You are a man rabbit.

Scene 77 : the ditch behind a chap's compost heap.

Jed: I am going to the bed shop. I need a bigger bed. The bed I have is not
big enough for my romps.
Bud: Your bed already fills your room.
Jed: I will go to the room shop and buy a bigger room. I need a bigger
romping room.
Bud: Your room is already bigger than the house.
Jed: I will go to the house shop and trade in my house for a huge
romping villa. I need room for future romp expansion.
Bud: Romps of the kind you engage in are the invention of Satan. He
invented them during his recreational period. Traditional sports and
exercises were not enough for him.
Jed: What I really need is a romping village. Or an island.
Bud: You are a man with a balloon for brains.

Scene 78: the bottom of a man's cage.

Bud: I just found a bunch of girl's under-things in the laundry I was going to do. Where did they come from?
Jed: Here and there.
Bud: I'll wash them separately on a delicates cycle.
Jed: You're a peach.
Bud: It looked like they did not all belong to the same girl. Some were petite while others were on the large side, to put it mildly.
Jed: You're right, Sherlock. I'm a great fan of Little and Large. And I am happy to say I'm not picky, either. My lady friends come in all shapes and sizes.
Bud: Lady friends in all shapes and sizes are the invention of Satan. He invented them when he wanted to find out if there was a line men would not cross, and when he found out there was no such line he was so pleased he left them to reproduce ad infinitum.
Jed: You didn't happen to see a latex man pouch in amongst those things did you? I seem to have misplaced mine.
Bud: You are Baboonaman

Scene 82: The closet in a man's closet.

Bud: That's a very fine evening gown.
Jed: Yes, it's dress up day at work.
Bud: You are beguiling, but in an unsettling way.
Jed: This is nothing. You should see what I'm wearing underneath.
Bud: I shudder to imagine. Also, I have a question. You can perhaps guess what it is.
Jed: As ever, guesswork is outside my skill set.
Bud: I was wondering what Betty would make of it.
Jed: This is Betty's gown. But they are Coco's under-things. They are such sexually mischievous girls. This was their idea.
Bud: Sexually mischievous girls with ideas are the invention of Satan. He invented them at the same time as sleepless nights and the torment of desires that can never be properly sated. And then he threw in free and easy-to-find pornography on the internet just to make the point.
Jed: I didn't think this was my colour, but Betty says pink loves me.
Bud: You are a man testing the limits of belief.

Chronicles

CHRONICLES (1)

I've been having a time. This is only my own
perspective but as far as I'm concerned it's the only
one that matters. No sooner had the plumber
fixed the faulty drainaway on the kitchen sink
than I accidentally cracked the coffee pot against
the tap while washing it and now I need to buy
a new coffee pot. But these are trivial concerns
compared to wondering whether or not it's too late
to begin reading all the great literature of the world
in chronological order taking the countries in
alphabetical order in cheap and affordable translations
where necessary and where readily available. The longer
I spend dawdling thinking about it the shorter the time
remaining to me. I'm not getting any younger and
I've always wanted to be well-read. I also wanted
a good memory so I could remember what I read
but it's not wise to wish for too much. That way
holds only disappointment and I've been having
such a time of it lately one doesn't dare to push
the gods too far. I'm sure it's they who are responsible
for everything around me becoming blurred to
such an extent I'm worrying about worrying if it's not
too late to read all the great literature of the world
before nurse comes one last time to close the drapes
and wish me a pleasant journey and she's sure
where I'm going I'll be comfortable and won't need
my reading glasses or those magazines I keep hidden.

CHRONICLES (2)

I've been having a time. I couldn't really afford
the cab fare although having only a 50/50 chance of
arriving in one piece is so exhilarating I figured
I could go without lunch just this once. Fear of death
subdues the appetite. I didn't know if she would be home
or not. I was bringing some pearl pies I baked
that had nothing in them except wisdom – it's a recipe
I thought she'd find talk-about-able. In the morning
the librarian had told me to obey the rules or lose my privileges.
I was so upset I snuck off and cried behind the bust
of Philip Larkin, I think it is. Or Churchill.
The day turned briefly into the kind of air
I've always found it so difficult to breathe.
As we sped through parts of town I don't like
it struck me how behind those curtains are secrets
they never told us about. It's all so much hokum
in my opinion. It's not for us to know what
thoughts lurk unseen in the minds of men and women.
Only yourself matters and not what other people do.
Anyway, such is the time I've been having of course
she wasn't home. I know how regret can flap its wings
and cast its shadow. I ate my own pies, thinking how
we could've sat together and watch the car park fall dark.

CHRONICLES (3)

I've been having a time. Today the shepherds
packed up the hillside and took it home.
They put the wool in special bags to keep it dry.
There was nothing left to do but take one last photograph.
And in the afternoon as the farm workers took a break
and sat in the shade of the trees to sip cooling drinks
and munch on candy bars I added a few lines
to the ode I'm working on and chucked out some of the lines
I added yesterday. To say that progress is slow
would be over-stating it. The thing about sheep is
they have no mind of their own and the other thing about sheep is
when they look at you it's as if they know what you're thinking
which is remarkable because they look absolutely blank
and couldn't care less and it's the accuracy of that blankness
and couldn't care less which is disturbing. When
evening came I realized there wasn't going to be a bus
through here again today and I was going to have to hitch a ride
or walk. Such is the time I've been having I walked.
As much as one admires this country
one can't deny its hidden dangers. I told myself to stay grounded.
In my head I added a few more words to my ode.
"If you come and live with me out there beyond the cesspit
and be my love
I'll arrange for the garbage to be taken away as often as possible.
If you come and live with me out there in the meadow under the blue sky
and be my love
I'll arrange for the weather to be always tolerable." I'm not sure
the ode is my forté. The jeremiad, on the other hand,
is even further beyond my range.
And by the time I arrived home you would've seen my socks
through the soles of my shoes if you'd taken a moment to look.

CHRONICLES (4)

I've been having a time. This morning
brought the revelation that while we were sleeping
someone had stolen our eggs. It was a mystery
for there was no sign of a break-in and all the doors and windows
were still secure. Limishka suggested the absence of eggs
could be explained by our having forgotten to buy any
but she has these crazy ideas and all you can do is humour her.
One day she will be old enough to know
what kind of a wicked world this really is.
Breakfast had to be forged from what scraps we could muster.
It reminded me of the days when I lived under the by-pass
and I was really having a time and all there was to eat
was the litter that blew in from the gas station
and all there was to drink were the tears of the woodland animals
who came to gaze upon me in my plight. Those days
didn't last long but I fear their return
and regret my neglect in making adequate provision for the future.
For a while today the world was completely silent
for there was nobody else nearby
and even the birds had ceased their song. The workmen
had abandoned their work and their machines stood silent
and there were no cars or buses or trucks on the road
and nobody sat outside on the grass chattering.
All would have been perfect had it not been
for a momentary dream brought on by too much pie at lunch.
I like to nap but fear its consequences in much the same way
as I fear waking up out of the night. You never know what's waiting.

CHRONICLES (5)

I've been having a time. Sunday, and one could
lay abed pondering life's vagaries, making
pathetic stabs at solving the annoying little puzzles
always popping up in front of you when all you want
is to go out and buy that beaver hat you saw yesterday
as the bus stopped outside the mall. Hold on to your ideals!
is what Dad used to say, but it's easier said than done.
When ennui manifests itself as a physical feeling
rather than a mental one, is that the time to
begin worrying? Someone knocked at the door today
but we didn't answer it because we didn't know
who it was and we don't feel like taking
any unnecessary chances. You only have
so many chances in this life and wasting them
would be foolish. Later, when the pig man came
for his money, he told us that there were people
going door-to-door offering cheap pork for sale
that was cat meat. He told us to be on our guard
but against what he did not say. I miss the old days
when what you had was always what you thought
it was. I wish we could bring back history. I wish
I still lived next door to my neighbours and not
those strangers in their invisibility cloaks and with
words of mystery that seem to mean everything
I don't understand and never shall. This afternoon
I had the kind of time I've been having of late:
there was thunder and lightning but no rain and
I stayed indoors watching television on my own.

CHRONICLES (6)

I've been having a time. I say stuff
but nobody seems to understand what I'm talking
about. I don't know what the problem is,
it's not like I'm talking in code
and I've never been mistaken for a Symbolist.
I don't even use metaphors. I canter
into the cake shop and ask for cake
and the girl behind the counter gives me
a long cold stare instead of a cake. It's enough
to make me run to my cupboard
and dismantle my cake collection and turn
to other self-gratifying pursuits. There are plenty
of alternatives. I've always been fascinated by
abstruse thinking so perhaps now's the time
to see if it's as much fun as it sounds
and annoying for other people. Today I could not
breathe. Limishka took a photograph of me
not breathing on her iPhone, there was bird flu
in the newspaper, and we're having nothing
to do with chickens or pigs. Our hope is
that our dreams will not become our chaos.
But I've been having such a time of it lately
all my plans are under review because they appear
to have not been properly thought through
and the outlook appears distressingly cloudy,
nobody understanding what it's like in here. So
I go to the cake shop to buy a cake and come home
with a look that would kill if you could only've seen it,
there's a persistent drizzle gracing the day
and at home one glance told me I should dust.

CHRONICLES (7)

I've been having a time. The rain's been coming
down in sheets and everyone seems to agree
happiness is always short-lived but perhaps the everyone
I consult with are the wrong peoples: scholars and
hair-trimmers and doctors and plate-bringers
and the man who fixes the plumbing or the electric
when it goes wrong. I've been looking for
a philosopher-king but so far I've not found one
although there are plenty of idiots making claims.
Then there's the poseur always dropping foreign *mots*
into English sentences. She studied Chinese
using the immersion method; if only the school had been
at sea, and she no swimmer. It's not people
I loathe but the masks and costumes people wear.
This afternoon I was crouching on the balcony
with my telescope trained on the balconies
of the building opposite to see
if I could catch anyone trifling with anyone's affections
behind the black sheets of rain and their drapes
so damp and listless. It's not the masks and costumes
people wear I loathe but the people, for
I've been having such a time of it lately
and I'm finding blame is easily apportioned.
Oh Limishka! Come to my rescue!
Too soon have you taken to your wings!
I saw you this morning tangled in the web of a spider
and spent the rest of the day imagining your struggles.

CHRONICLES (8)

I've been having a time. The curling leaves
of my book suggest something but the air is
so heavy it's taking a long time for us to decide upon
anything and what the curling leaves suggest
will have to wait until later. Let's wait
for the ink to dry, the underwear to dry, the bed
linen to dry, your eyes to dry before we decide upon
what to do next. Perhaps also there is
a hint of deceit lurking in the air but no-one
is owning to it. I've been feeling more ironic
than usual, and everything in Nature
positively drips with God and Godliness
so tonight (after I finish this) we will go night-fishing,
a nocturnal activity that seems to be
all the go with the youth. Here, this being the seaside,
you can capture more unsuspecting fishes
and aquatic creatures than a body would believe.
I'm not sure they are all edible
but whatever: we eat them anyway
and deal with the food poisoning later.
My best friend's best friend works in a pharmacy
so we get a discount on over-the-counter medicines
and free advice. Once (I'd been having
something of a time if truth be told)
he suggested I go fuck myself, and I did.

CHRONICLES (9)

I've been having a time. This morning we
went to the ladder shop but the only ladders
they had went down, they didn't have any
going up, and we left empty-handed. At lunchtime
the greens were turned yellow and the beans
had been beans but by the time we reached them
they'd given up being beans a long time ago.
And it turns out my jokes are not funny anymore
even though I steal most of them
from some of history's greatest funny men.
This afternoon during my guitar lesson
it dawned on me that what I was holding
was not a guitar but a dream and to hold on to a dream
was too clichéd even for a tired dreamer
and so I abandon the guitar as I have abandoned
so many things - the wives, the lovers,
the gift of prophecy being the most easily remembered.
You would think by now I would have seen
the time I've been having coming
but I'm going nuts, to be honest,
and blind to the obvious,
and I only notice the bleeding obvious
when the blood can no longer be ignored.

CHRONICLES (10)

I've been having a time. Compared to
a herd of stampeding buffalo I think
what we are experiencing here is a walk in a garden
where two butterflies are flying together
near the buddleia but I have been known to be wrong
and while there's been a shift in emphasis
the basics remain the same: the boss says he wants me to
be a slave driver but I'm more of a natural tidier-upper
owing to my blood being all Virgo
and my inclination being pretty much to be
the driven. But I'm thinking of resigning
and taking another trip to another world
as if the blue sky has all the answers. You know
every day is the same from beginning to end,
it's like you get the same tedious email every day
but you still have to read it because it's the Law
and the Law must be obeyed. It's all so much bunkum
when all we want is to go home and have sex with someone
and if not sex then some serious play. But
I've been having such a time of it lately
even that seems too much of a shemozzling. Anyway,
today's "news" is that thanks to a slice of pie
that slipped off my plate on to the canteen floor
at lunchtime I'm now no longer on speaking terms
with Abigail Someone who runs Nature Club.

CHRONICLES (11)

I've been having a time. The wall
outside continues to grow and the bricks
carry on being delivered. This morning the wake up
bird in the tree outside our window was singing
about how it's good to not be in so much
of a hurry for the future will come soon enough.
I don't know where he finds his feathery wisdom.
I don't know if he ever lets his feet touch the ground.
Be that as it all may, this morning also
saw the return of the self-support stocking: I believed
it was gone for ever and indeed it did not stay
long this time around either but sometimes a short time
is time enough. But don't assume too much
pleasure for the time I've been having
is still with me. The sun may rise of a morning
but rest assured it's scurried behind
the clouds before the breakfast things
have been cleared away. Later in the May day
after I had seen a man beating a woman
I searched for someone to interpret what I had been
hearing using my ears. It was a language from
the factory where they make the mouths
people use who do not want to say anything to upset
anyone else. They are another species
and as different from my kind as my kindness is
different from my insensitivity.

CHRONICLES (12)

I've been having a time. Today the gardeners
came to cut the weeds we call a lawn
and they spent more time smoking cigarettes
than gardening so it's no little wonder
we are living in a wildness that can drive a brain
into confusion. Workmen are building a road
where a road doesn't need to go
while the river carries its filth in a never-ending stream
from garbage heap to garbage heap although
here they call them development zones and sometimes
towns. The gardeners took time off from
smoking their cigarettes to watch the river
carry its filth etc. Meanwhile, I read
the sixth chapter of *East of Eden*
to take my mind off living in an under-developed
country. Tomorrow I will probably read chapter seven
because I'm determined to make it through to
fifty-five, being myself well on the way to sixty-one.
It's not that age bothers me so much
as it drives me to distraction. Today I even considered
writing an ode to the effect that my distraction
is entering a new phase, a phase as yet un-named
but which I shall probably call Henry
for I've been having such a time of it lately
making sense is proving the least of my concerns.

CHRONICLES (13)

I've been having a time. Most weeks
I don't know what month or the day it is.
I'm gonna have to move apartment!
I'm gonna have to get in a box and conceal my parts!
I'm gonna have to talk to a real girl
where once an imaginary girl cast a shadow.
But I'm gonna refuse her sex. I'm gonna
pretend she's a marble statue
on a pedestal in the lobby of a library.
This morning I wilted under the fire of her smile.
Soon I'm going to have to meet her folks
because this afternoon we had a cup of silent tea
in the Marigold Tea Rooms. This can only
lead to complications. The next thing you know
we'll be on first name terms. Lately
I've been having such a time I had to
have my watch examined in the watch shop.
They checked the battery and the magnetism
and I have both of those okay. I don't
go on dates, and I fall asleep at night
imagining another life, a life fractionally
more exciting than this one. And before I wake
all kinds of things can happen, and then
when I awaken all I can think is how it was fun
but then I had to look for clean clothes
and I was behind on the laundry as usual.

CHRONICLES (14)

I've been having a time. Many a time
lately I've found myself
awash with regret at not having learned
to swim. As the metaphorical water-level rises
around me and symbolic fish flap by
(how politely they flap their fins
in greeting!) I wonder if they know
I'm drowning. I'm drowning
and clutching a broken gamp in quiet despair.
It's rainy season here.
I have been drawn to predatory fish in the past
and have suffered some bites.
This morning as the tropical sun surrendered
to the tropical clouds and the wind
and darkness at noon fell upon our brows
you could have found me
if you would have found me
treading hackneyed waters. I've been having
a time, it's as if the Navigation Acts
(whatever they are)
apply only to me, and if I knew
how to negotiate these waters so nobody saw me
that would cheer me up a little, I think.

CHRONICLES (15)

I've been having a time. Outside my window
the world has all kinds of voices but an argument
outside my window at 6.45 in the morning
is a voice I'd rather not hear. And of the people
lining up in the air to speak with me
the number I want to talk with is between
zero and two. Checking the enthusiasm cupboard
I see the shelves are almost empty.
I'm sleepy as hell.
I can't keep my eyes open.
I've been like this all day and I'm in danger of
losing my job with the alarm company.
Lunchtime, in pursuit of an excellent sausage,
all I could find was a disfigured girl selling
hastily-daubed self-portraits. You can't live
on self-portraits. And the noise of traffic
is getting me down, I'm thinking of moving
to the middle of nowhere if I can locate it.
They say it's beyond the ills. I think they mean
hills, but I've been having such a time of late
I don't care what they mean. I stopped
listening to them a long time ago. All I hear
these days is the little voice in my head,
irritating beyond measure, filled with truths.

CHRONICLES (16)

I've been having a time. It's important to look
good from not only the front but the back too,
but it's not always possible and anyway
what's there and what people see is not always
the same thing. Oh, it's been such a time of late,
and the astrolabe can no longer be relied upon
to identify a good time for prayer, as if prayer
holds the answer to the ills of such times. But
today it was impossible to be too gloomy: Andy
reminded me of Schuyler's gull coasting by
"as unexpected as a kiss on the nape of the neck"
and I reminded myself of what it is to be alive.
It's so easy to forget amidst all this grief, but
Limishka yearns for my kiss on the nape of her neck.
Today at 5.45 I planted that kiss and the rising sun
cast its light on the sleepy buildings opposite. It looked
like a good drying day: I was tempted to hang out
my laundry in this poem, but resisted as I resist
the temptation to be dull. My work is not scholarly.
I'm sort of having a chat with myself, I think
you could say. And this evening as I lounged
considering tomorrow I was in no hurry to be there.
The mosquitoes were hunting in packs but the day
had been fine. Tomorrow will have its critics
and I don't care how closely they scrutinize my doings.

CHRONICLES (17)

I've been having a time. But
other people are having more of a time
and my own shrinks into the shadows of inconsequence
by comparison. Each day Limishka
goes to work and faces what is for her
the daunting rock climb of the world's impossible demands,
impossible because she does not belong to the world;
she has her own. And David has come back
from the hospital bearing bad news
and looks set to join the list of dearest friends
taken too soon. So much for the time I've been having;
reality will insist on gate-crashing the party. Why can't life
be how we want it to be rather than the way it is?
Today there was a Red Storm Warning
and classes were cancelled
and I sat here blank as the day is blank
watching the incessant rain and drinking too much coffee.
At lunchtime Limishka cried
all over the phone, and then I had eggs and sausage
because whatever is happening you have to eat.
But I had no stomach for it.
I don't want to lose any more people.

CHRONICLES (18)

I've been having a time. June arrives
and her long days trail listlessly in her wake and her
long days beckon untrustworthily before her. June's days
are everywhere now: on the dead branches of
the neglected tree, among the tufts of weed
on the neglected lawns, in the palms of the hands
of the inconstantly shiftless suffocating
breathless airs. The shoes I bought yesterday
are too large. I'm falling over every time I take a step
whether it be forward or back. And my hat is constantly falling
over my eyes; I think my head is shrinking. But
I tell myself don't fuss. I'm alright, and falsification of
the evidence is appropriate; this has always been my strong point.
Summer is arrived and driving a fiery coach and horses
through our every breath. This evening in town
the bees were queuing up to get into the bar.
It was a bar-bee-queue and also a joke I made up. But
such is the time I've been having most of
what I encounter is akin to a blessing of falling glass
and would we were sheltered from any further grace.

CHRONICLES (19)

I've been having a time. There is such a thing
as being blessed by falling glass. There are wishes
that stretch the soul. There will be days that see no night
and lately it's been kind of sitting here waiting
for them to arrive if not for oneself then
for someone else. Last night wings were flapping while we slept
and this morning I noticed an increase in the level of wastage.
Suction pumps interrupt my songs, and not far away
a factory is adrift from its moorings, its chains
broken asunder. Such is the time. This afternoon
a message arrived from our neighbour and it was the usual
niceties preceding complaints and negativity verging on abuse.
A saving grace is that he is a fool, and wears
the fool's hat and terribly sensible shoes. If society falls
apart, as they predict, no-one will notice his absence
as we sort through the debris. That reminds me:
we could do with a new broom.

CHRONICLES (20)

I've been having a time. The doors of the asylum
have become unhinged until every word
we say matters. From the tree opposite our balcony
this morning the song of an infectious chaffinch
(that is, the infectious song of) spoke of
the love affair between eternal foes. It makes you think.
It makes you think how you may tolerate
the intolerable because at least it speaks of life
even if it's un-understandable, or mis-understandable.
Wind blew and blew. The drying clothes changed
from hanging in the vertical to flying in the horizontal.
We decided our trip to the man-made island
where birds have to be flown in specially
should be postponed. Instead and inconsequentially
we visited the pharmacy. It's possible to
have a time in a pharmacy, and I did. Some people
are born monotonous and stay that way, night and day
and Sunday and all. It occurred to me
as Limishka looked for skin cream and shampoo
how one can look into the eyes of anyone and find there a story
and that I have no interest in any of them.

CHRONICLES (21)

I've been having a time. There is this
or nothing left to say about the matter.
Dreamed a special announcement from my sponsor
to the effect that current uncertainties will now extend
well into the future, and even beyond. Limishka,
take my hand and accompany me. Oh, how I
sat by the window this morning and wrote those words
and how I sat in the path of an oncoming bus
this evening recalling them. Before I was dragged.
To. Safety. And oh, it may well be that imaginings
have more import than actual events.
Lunchtime I clocked a police cadet wandering lost in a mall.
Lunchtime I was offered "watchees" in a mall.
Lunchtime we were lost in a mall.
It was of no matter: it was raining outside and inside
was better. Slightly. I noticed a lot of people
looking at us as if we were some kind of show.
I looked back. I stood in the accessories shop and looked
back at two men staring at me. They looked away.
It's like this. Somebody without a face may be
listening to this or reading this or ignoring this totally.

CHRONICLES (22)

I've been having a time. Walking backwards
clapping my hands doesn't seem to have made
much difference. Being nice to people
I don't like hasn't made any difference at all.
Eating a good breakfast has made no difference.
Eschewing the dubious pleasures of too much wine
has made a difference but I'm still
having a time. Putting my faith in the god of poetry
was never going to make a difference
and it never will. I tried switching it around and
going with the poetry of God but
that seemed to make things worse so I hauled back
fast as the camel would allow. This time
of the year the snow accumulates and no
amount of blazing sunshine will make it go away.
There's so much of not making much difference.
The garbage lorry just roared by
and I thought for no good reason
of a chap from my ancient history who said he had some shoes
exactly like mine except his were brown not black
and they had a buckle across the instep instead of laces.
I want someone to bring me ham
wrapped in a cabbage leaf, but that isn't going to happen
and it makes no difference
if sweet are the uses of adversity and then
perhaps all this is okay after all. The end
of the book is approaching, after all.

JUNE CHRONICLES (23)

I've been having a time. Someone
knocked on my day and ran away, they took my banners,
I heard their footsteps on the stairs;
probably it was an old woman
with some kind of complaint, but can old women run?
Anyway, back to gardening,
and you know what happens
when you tumble head-first into the rhubarb patch?
Yes. And it's no good claiming other people's footsteps
dog your own. We control our shoes,
or we should. It was a sunny day, hot and sleepy.
But the fish is only sleepy because it partakes
of its owner's personality.
I forget what I just did. What I said. The thing.
It's a trap!
Oh yes -
it's a trap sure enough, and we're falling in.
Then, because I've been having a time, it's suddenly all haywire
and the blues comes. Well,
circumstances permitting
we're gonna try sculpting the future
and don't care what those bastards think.

Appendices

APPENDIX 1: HOW I WROTE "WHY I AM ALWAYS PEEKING OVER MY SHOULDER"

First I thought of the title. Well, I didn't exactly think of it, but the title appeared in my mind and almost immediately I thought it was an okay title although when it appeared I didn't know for sure it was going to be a title it was just a phrase but anyway I tried to remember it until I could find a pencil. I found a pencil and then wrote it down. By this time I had decided it was definitely a title, and it was "Why I Am Always Peeking Over My Shoulder".

The first four words of the poem ("Umbrella complicate of tree-house") arrived (from where I cannot say with any certainty) at around the same time as an urgent, surprising and acute but thankfully short-lived attack of diarrhea occasioned I think by some untrustworthy seafood. I wrote them down on a napkin, because I am of the generation that does that kind of thing. Uses napkins, I mean.

I did not understand the words. Or to be more precise: I understood each word but I didn't understand why they were together holding hands like girls in a mall. Anyway, I left them as they were because they seemed literary and "open to interpretation", like Dan Brown's novels. They're not quite a real sentence, and because I adore grammar I put a dash at the end instead of a full-stop or a comma or something else.

With this much under my belt the time had come to decide if this was going to be a long poem or a short poem, obscure or anecdotal, ambiguous or popular. I have to admit that decisions of this nature are usually determined by the state of my life at the time: if I'm happy or sad, bored or non-committal, having frequent sexual intercourse, or in the middle of my annual "I should read The Bible" period. As it happened, I had recently brought to a close a pleasant but fruitless period of solitude (I had planned to write my masterpiece, but it didn't happen) and re-entered the world of woe by renting a dilapidated, nay ruined, apartment in an area ripe for gentrification albeit within earshot of aircraft taking off and landing, and taken a part-time job as a KFC delivery boy. An experience during that time perhaps explains the next line of the poem:

> I'm threatened. Girl horror, I didn't see the knife

Of course, I had to decide if this line really "worked" with the "Umbrella complicate of tree-house" line but those kind of tough decisions are what poets are faced with every day of their seemingly interminable lives.

But from here on it was easy; the final line gave me no trouble at all. It was as if invisible hands were guiding my own hands as they sped over the keys of the keyboard. I may even have been asleep.

It's quite a short poem (only three lines) and looking back at it now from a long distance I wonder if the title and the first line and the second line and, I guess, the last line are at all connected in any useful and comprehensible way but I think language is like a fish you can't keep a hold of and I really think after a few drinks it's possible to see the poem as a self-sufficient object, which is more than can be said most of the time about almost anything. I think if I were given the chance to revise it I might change some of the words, but since it's been published I think it's too late. But "umbrella" is not quite right, and neither is "complicate". I'm not too sure about the "tree-house" either. And I never really liked "They called the fictitious luminary I blurry stared into the starry starry light & in the passage-way-cum-shelter O unbecoming beauty but never quite sad enough to be considered an alarming case such circumstance and so examined but if and also the bird on bough was falling into angel's terminus or maybe that was only in a dream and whether or not rising death rates or falling in love of course we are not machines but threatened by annexation and examination O life expectancy how nature tricks and however it is it is isn't it, a rhetorical question", because now I can see it's definitely much too long. I don't know how come I didn't pick up on that at the time.

APPENDIX 2: A TEST FOR POETS

1. What is your first thought when you wake up in the morning?
2. Would you rather be a pop star than a poet?
3. What is the best time of day to write a poem?
4. What role does the ego have to play in the art of poetry?
5. Does poetry matter?
6. Is there such a thing as a Poetry Establishment?
7. Can the craft of poetry be learned?
8. Does poetry need a subject?
9. Do you remember the first poem you ever wrote?
10. Is it better for the poet to be
>   (a) unrecognized
>   (b) underrated
>   (c) unknown
>   (d) undressed
11. Is it reasonable that many of our "best" poets are actually no good?
12. Is the internet a kind of poetry?
13. Which of the following best approximates to the distance between the poems you wanted to write and the poems you have written?
>   (a) a couple of inches
>   (b) a mile
>   (c) from here to eternity
>   (d) more than words can say
14. Is your poetry too personal?
15. Is poetry sociable?
16. Have you ever dreamed a marvellous poem only to find it was gone upon waking?
17. In which of the following periods was it a joy to be a poet?
>   (a) the Elizabethan Age
>   (b) the 1950s
>   (c) the Thatcher years
>   (d) last weekend
18. Is it possible to be original?
19. When you write a poem do you discover a larger better version of yourself?
20. Is self-doubt important for the poet?
21. Are you sure?
22. Is there any subject unfit for poetry?
23. Look at the following drawing. Do you see
>   (a) a horse
>   (b) the Taj Mahal
>   (c) Manet's Olympia
>   (d) the poet laureate   [choose one]
24. In which city is it best to be a poet?
25. Are your poems in colour or black and white?

26. How do you usually feel when you hear other poets read their work?

    (a) uninterested

    (b) depressed

    (c) suicidal

    (d) elsewhere   {tick as appropriate}

27. Did you ever count syllables whilst writing a poem and, if so, do you now realize it was a mistake?

28. Is it possible to be both a poet and a nice person?

29. How many times have you given up on poetry?

30. How many times has poetry given up on you?

31. Which weather is best suited to the writing of poetry?

    (a) summer calm

    (b) autumn mists

    (c) typhoon

    (d) sunshine and showers

32. For whom do you write?

33. Is poetry the same as real life?

34. Is poetry these days a young man's game? Or a young woman's?

35. Do you have any idea what the poets in Ghana are doing these days?

36. Do you think anyone really understands what you write?

37. Is the maintaining of a healthy diet and a clean and ethically sound lifestyle important if the upcoming 21st century poet is to be "taken up" by the Poetry Establishment?

38. Should a poet dress

    (a) fashionably

    (b) eccentrically

    (c) what might best be described as "neutrally"

39. How may a poet tell when they have "peaked"?

40. At what age should one retire from poetry and bow out gracefully?

41. What is the difference between a poet and an undertaker?

42. Is the culling of poets the way forward?

43. Has the idea of "influence" had any influence on your writing, and do you think you have influenced other writers?

44. A propos Question 43, has the evil of plagiarism ever disturbed your tranquility?

45. How many friends do you have?

46. Has poetry had its day and, if so, what day was it?

47. Do you think your poems will continue to live when you don't?

48. What is your last thought before you fall asleep at night?

49. Do you sleep well?

50. What's for dinner?

1. "A force for good is only a good thing if it doesn't use too much force and if it really is good." Paddy Crake, from *A Summation Of Recent Thoughts*, Parse, London, 2012.

2. *Carousel*, by Richard Rodgers and Oscar Hammerstein II, especially the songs *"If I Loved You"*, *"June Is Bustin' Out All Over"* and *"You'll Never Walk Alone"*.

3. Milton's *Journals* (browsed whilst listening to Kanye West)

4. "Once of a lifeless form we were, an army drawn to sleepy girls, flamed of passion but torn from arms, as once our boys were ripped from sight." (Anonymous)

5. "The hair of the ocean is the most marvellous of hairs." Jeremy Twill, from *Organs to Grind* (1998)

6. "The uses to which mule skin can be put are too many to enumerate here, but some examples are gloves, masks, handbags, book covers, knee protectors, decorative coverings for furniture (coffee tables, dumb waiters etc), uniforms for dumb waiters, condoms (old school style), hats for boys, and the lining of vanity cases." from *The Skinner's Handbook*, Cambridge, 1987.

7. Geoffrey Chaucer, *The Canterbury Tales*

8. Malcolm Shirt in conversation with Peggy Herzegovina in *Root Vegetable Monthly*. In particular, what he has to say about growing his own carrots e.g. "I like them young and fresh."

9. Samuel Taylor Coleridge, *"A Letter To (Sara Hutchinson)"* & *"Dejection: An Ode"*

10. "Do not punish fear; cherish it." Bibby Carew, from *The Eleven Commandments*, Bibby's Books, Sacramento, 2002.

11. "The days pass and here I am always in the same worldly abyss." from *The Diary of St. Gemma Galgani, 1878-1903*

12. Constance Small, *The Complete Romances (abridged for young readers)*, Ladybug Books (1999)

13. "On every first weekend of the month the Concord town elders held a dance. It was very popular with the youth because of the free lemonade. I never went, dance not being my thing. But Thoreau went every time." Ralph Waldo Emerson, *Memoirs*.

14. "The work being cleared out of the way by the Workers, Mrs. Livingston read from the Bible out in the open, with the girls sitting on the ground with feet tucked under them. Overhead the birds sang sweetly, their voices heard even above those of the girls when all joined in the singing that followed the reading of the Scriptures." Janet Aldridge, from *The Meadow-Brook Girls Under Canvas*, Henry Altemus Company, Philadelphia, 1913

15. "Our names describe our potential and our names limit us. I will never forgive my parents for naming me Judith." Bingo Kramer, from *My Life in the Tree Behind Our House* (Autopsy Publications, Tilehurst, 1984)

16. Michel de Montaigne, *The Complete Essays*, Penguin (1987)

17. "Blessed is the man who, having nothing to say, abstains from giving wordy evidence of the fact." George Eliot, from *Impressions of Theophrastus Such*, 1879

18. "Rain arose a smile, the bow of pleasure; how many times have we engaged upon the breeze-blown grass?" Alberta Stereo, from *Spring and Its Games* (Isi-Isi-Yesiyis, Reykjavik, 1991)

19. "Let us pause a moment and consider where we are and, before we pause, let's wait a while and think about how we came to be here. Some of us took a train, others only woke up and discovered somehow their place had been decided for them. What discoveries they had unwittingly passed by! And then some have been dragged here by people who know what's good for them. It never ceases to confound our leaders how no matter how many signs one puts up anarchy reigns." Constantine Pope, from *Some Thoughts Provoked by Gazing Too Long at a Wall* (The Chic Organization, New York, 2013)

20. John Ashbery, "*Daffy Duck in Hollywood*"

21. "Apart we can be stronger. That will confound them." The Doo-Wops, *Baby Let's Go!*

22. "Let us stop a moment and think about where we are and, before we stop, let's pause a while and consider how we came to be here. Some of us took a tram, others only woke up and discovered somehow their place had been decided for them. What discoveries they had unwittingly passed by! And then some have been dragged here by people who know what's good for them. It never ceases to confound our organizers that no matter how many signs are put up apostasy reigns." Constantine Pope, from *Some Thoughts Provoked by Gazing Too Long at a Boy* (The Chic Organization, New York, 2013)

23. John Keats, "*To Autumn*"

24. The Information Age: " ..... the very notion of our actions, our endeavors and especially our mistakes, being perfectly archived is somewhat terrifying to say the least...." (Someone, somewhere, sometime; you can Google it.)

25. "The woeful sun, slowly fading behind the clouds of an ever brewing storm, so nearly impossible, yet slowly the pallbearer ...." etc. etc. Pauline Larkin, from *Sorrow and Extinction* (Witty Books, Brighton, 1999)

26. Frank O'Hara, "*A City Winter*"

27. "His oft repeated experience of body sensation converting to dream image marks Coleridge's dream theory with a sharp 'psychosomatic' awareness, an adjective he coins to describe the delicate permeability existing between the body's sensations and the mind's emotions and images. Coleridge also develops the term 'double touch' to name this ability of the body to feel itself, to tell by means of the organ of the skin what is ME and NOT ME." Kathryn Kimball, from *Coleridge's Dream Theory and the Dual Imagination*, (Coleridge Bulletin, New Series 16, Winter 2000)

28. Kenneth Koch, *The Burning Mystery of Anna in 1951* (Random House, 1979)

29. "It will be good when the leaves on the trees return." Cubby Woods, *A Year in the Forest* (Abracazoom Eco-Chapbooks Series XV, Volume IV, Epping, 2002)

30. Thanks also go to The Psychic Medium Team. They can advise you on any issue you have. They offer relaxed and calm readings with experienced spiritual readers who are non-judgmental and there to advise you 24 hours a day. Call on 0904 007 0213 - it's only 46p per minute.

Lightning Source UK Ltd.
Milton Keynes UK
UKOW04f1308081215

264339UK00001B/1/P